SALMON IN THE SEINE

Alaskan Memories of Life, Death, & Everything In-Between

NORRIS COMER

MILSPEAK BOOKS

An imprint of MilSpeak Foundation, Inc.

Manufactured in the United States of America

Library of Congress Cataloging-in-Publication Data

Comer, Norris

Library of Congress Control Number: 2021947299
ISBN 978-1-7378676-2-3 (paperback)
ISBN 978-1-7378676-6-1 (epub)

Editing by: M.C. Armstrong
Cover art by: www.BoldBookCovers.com
Formatting by: www.BoldBookCovers.com

MilSpeak Foundation, Inc.
5097 York Martin Road
Liberty, NC 27298
www.MilSpeakFoundation.org

CONTENTS

ACKNOWLEDGMENTS

The acknowledgments section of a published work that intimately details the lives of real people and places, like *Salmon in the Seine*, is crucial in its own unique way. Dire, even. An author who is granted access to an insular community such as the commercial fishing fleet of Cordova, Alaska, and does not at least tip his or her hat to the Real who made the storytelling possible—the human beings with their dizzying dreams and red viscera—is a proper bastard in my estimation. A betrayer. The outsider who was let inside because he or she was thought an exception to the shunned mainstream only to fail and further buttress cultural barricades.

So it is in the spirit of humility, respect, and love that I salute the ferociously alive coastal communities of Prince William Sound (with a favorable gaze to Cordova). Ultimately, this book is told as true to life as I could tell it, but inevitably I bet some of you in this story would've told it different. I ask you understand I also lived that summer 2008 and I get to tell it my way too. It is because of this humility, respect, and love that I changed the names of most of the characters and vessels to protect privacy. A few exceptions exist, for example Osa Schultz, Mike Webber, and the *Time Bandit* for whom the record (respectively *Exxon Valdez*-related Congressional testimony, journalistic citation, and television reference) demands.

With deference to the old African saying about taking a village to raise a child, I add that it takes a planet to publish a book. I first thank Tracy Crow.

Tracy's unwavering mentorship since my college days writing for the Eckerd College student newspaper *The Current* to championship as my literary agent, and now publisher, is nothing short of incredible. Frankly, it is hard to imagine this book coming together without her, who I refer to as the friendliest pit bull I know. Author and copyeditor Dr. Matt C. Armstrong's insightful comments and encouragement were also vital. I owe him a debt of thanks for he is a fine writer and teacher.

The MilSpeak Foundation and its donors must take a bow. Beyond the embrace of my book are the Foundation's tireless efforts to elevate the literary works of veterans and their families, a vital endeavor for America in this era marked by Forever War. Thank you, MilSpeak, for all that you do.

On a personal note, I thank my parents—Donald Comer and Dr. Heidi Nelson—for sacrificing so much to provide both a loving safe harbor and the encouragement to cast off the dock lines. My little sister Amelia Comer is to thank for helping me keep a foot in the world of childlike wonder. I shudder to think of what my life would be without you all.

Finally, I'd like to thank America and its people. I was born in 1989, the year the Soviet Union collapsed and when America seemed poised to have it all. What happened? The decades since are marked by traumas: 9/11 and the aforementioned Forever War Era; The Great Recession and ascendant American oligarchy; domestic authoritarian threats from all quarters; climate change leading to my beloved Pacific Northwest homeland smashing heat records and lighting ablaze; pandemic tragedy and horrific continued decrease of our national average lifespan; and more, more, more. Throughout it all, everyone with a pen from edgy cosmopolitan satirists to mainstream journalists have blamed The American. It is we, too stupid and too violent and too insert-flaw-here, causing all this suffering.

Well, I declare it here and now—I do not blame us. I'm aghast that the contemporary American writer appears to have largely forsaken The

American, often for a cheap price no less. No, we need our writers to champion our common cause. The horrors we face are from the top-down, failures belonging to the unaccountable few calling the shots who at the time of this writing give taxpayer subsidies to each other for joyrides in near orbit.

To The American, I dedicate this story with all the love I can muster. We're in this boat together, so to speak. We'll need one another more than ever in the years to come to endure the blows that define the times—like fishery collapsing oil spills and medical bankruptcy to which this book bears witness.

E. pluribus Unum.

PROLOGUE – MAN AND FISH

I covered the dying fisherman with a blanket, his right arm ripped off save a stubborn bicep a lifetime in the making. The blanket was adorned with action portraits of Spider-Man. Not my first choice of design for the occasion, but it'd have to do. Blood fast painted the deck of his boat where generations of salmon met similarly gruesome yet more profitable ends. His lips turned blue and skin maggoty white as his body shunted blood from the extremities to the core to prolong vital function. Being hypovolemic like this, going into shock, precludes death by trauma.

I didn't know any of this at the time. I was an eighteen-year-old greenhorn up from Oregon trying to make a buck in Alaska. One day throwing my graduation cap in the air, the next lying with good intention to a dying man about the promising ETA of a rescue chopper out of Anchorage. I knelt after elevating his feet with a family size box of Cheerios. His left hand found mine and clenched it palm-to-palm. His grip was strong. I squeezed back.

"You are a tough motherfucker, do you hear me?" I half-yelled. "You're the toughest guy I've ever met. You have to live, think of your son! Don't you go dying on him, you got that? Don't you dare! The chopper is going to be here any minute. You're going on that fucking thing to the hospital."

We were surrounded on deck by a group of good Samaritans. One with a radio relayed, "The father is almost back. Senior."

"Don't let my son see!" the fisherman howled. "Don't let him see me like this!"

"We won't let him see any of this," I said. "You have my word." To the man with the radio, I said, "His eleven-year-old son is aboard that boat. He was with us the whole season but got on a few hours ago with his grandpa to get a ride back to Cordova to start school."

Somebody whispered, "Christ." The skipper applying pressure on the wounded fisherman's nearly amputated arm shook his head.

"Why don't I quit?" the wounded fisherman groaned. His head shook side to side like it had a will of its own. He let go of my hand and shielded his face in the crook of his elbow. "Why don't I just fuckin' quit?"

"Nobody is quittin' nothin'," someone said in response.

Memory has formed into perspective since that summer of 2008. The way I see it, we live and die like the fish we slaughter, born of salt and blood and sperm and egg; a seething profane ooze of seawater and cum and rot and outer space and somehow, *life*. When the time comes, we journey from our home stream into the awe and horror of the sea, and the survivors in turn offer salt and blood and sperm and egg when given the chance. Despite our best efforts, the great net entraps us somewhere along the way and ultimately kills us. Cross the River Styx. Walk with Jesus in the light of our Lord. Drink mead with the warriors of Valhalla. Decompose into soil. I don't care what story you choose, the great net takes us there, guided by fate or chance— again, differing explanations for the same result—and we, half-swimming and half-pushed, find ourselves in the company of friends, lovers, and enemies charging forward to create life and die.

What drives the great net? asked the first philosopher on the African savanna, undoubtedly with different words and analogy as he or she looked to the stars and a goat's throat was slit for sacrifice. But I am telling a fisherman's story, so this is how I will interpret the world. Man is fish. Fish is man. The great net has us in its silent webbing, which is not so much an insightful epiphany as my limited view of the truth. We know heaven like salmon know the crooning apes who kill them for profit. For all I know, God is a fisherman with bills to pay.

Alaska Bound

I did not yet think man is fish and fish is man as the Boeing 747 jetted north from the tarmac of Portland International Airport to Alaska. I craned my neck from my aisle seat to glimpse out the window. The emerald swaths of Pacific Northwest conifers and the Cascade Mountain sentinels the likes of Mt. Hood and Mt. Rainier passed without ceremony.

"What more should I know about fishing before I get there, Cap'n Bryon?" I asked my newly met travel companion who sat in the middle seat next to me. The big-eyed, cherubic face of the eight-year-old tilted to the side before he stretched a tiny hand to play with the air valves above his seat. His mother was half-asleep and twisted into a barely tolerable position at the window. I didn't blame her. Little Bryon was a nonstop talker. He was great.

"My dad caught the hugest halibut last season," Bryon said, changing the subject. "Like, 5,000 pounds." His camo baseball hat threatened to slide off the back of his head and I gave the brim a quick tug to secure it back in place. Bryon squirmed against his low sitting seatbelt, face simmering with insult.

"Your daddy sounds like quite the fisherman," I indulged.

"Yah, he is. He said we're gonna go shoot'n too!" Bryon lifted his toy boat and flew it through the air while making *pew pew pew* laser noises.

1

"Don't bother the nice man, sweetie," Bryon's mom asked in the tired, dignified way of a gentle mother. She had short silver hair and looked at the two of us sleepily from behind thick-frame glasses. Her black fleece jacket was modest, her form petite beneath.

"It isn't a bother," I said. "Cap'n Bryon is teaching me how to fish, isn't that right Cap'n?" Bryon nodded.

"My dad, he took me out, and and, we saw whales. Big whales!" Bryon stretched his arms so that he touched both his mother and me.

"Wowza, probably part of the humpback migration or something, huh?" I said.

"No, this big!" Bryon insisted. Cap'n Bryon was only interested in his zoological identification system: *REALLY EFFING BIG WHALES*.

"Huge," I whispered in awe. "Like a T-rex." Bryon's mother smiled.

"You've been keeping my grandson busy the whole flight," she said and leaned in close with an edge to her gaze. "Thank you," she mouthed.

"Grandson? All this time I thought you were his mother," I said. She laughed at that one. "I'm Norris," I offered my hand. She took it gently, her hands boney and cold.

"Norris? I'm Sheryl Lippincott, it's a pleasure to meet you." Sheryl's smile broadened, then faded as she wedged back into the corner between her seat and the side of the airplane. Bryon chomped off the heads of his goldfish crackers, a lover of catching, killing, and eating fish in both flesh and cheese form. He offered me a cracker. I took it.

"Thanks, Cap'n," I said. I bit off the head with a dry crunch like how Bryon ate his. I felt Sheryl study me from the window.

"You're good with kids," she said. I swallowed.

"Well, I got a little sister you see. She's eight like Bryon and probably my favorite person there is. She even started a bacon fan club with a bunch of her little friends. They dress in pig masks and pray to the pig god and his

2

delicious gifts before their meetings. It feels vaguely culty? And Pacific Islander? I dunno, it's awesome," I hung on the verge of a tangent. Sheryl blinked.

"I see. Where in Alaska are you heading?"

"Cordova to work on a salmon seiner," I said. I took my last sip of ginger ale with tequila-shot gusto and stuffed an empty wrapper of courtesy biscuits in the iceless cup. Sheryl's brows rose.

"We're going to Cordova, too. We go up every summer. That's where Bryon's daddy, Dale, lives," she said.

"Are you guys commercial?" I asked. Sheryl shook her head.

"No, we just love it up there. Where are you from?"

"I'm from Oregon, Portland area," I said. "Lake Oswego, if that means anything to you. I just got out of high school and I'm taking a year off before college. Some people call it a Gap Year. Have you heard of it?" Sheryl nodded. "Anyway, when it came time to graduate I knew I had a year before college, but I didn't know how to make money to travel with. I went around to my teachers and asked them, 'How do I make money?' And they all gave me the same face—" I scrunched up my nose and cocked my brow at the same time, "—and said, 'We are high school teachers, we don't know how to make money!'" Sheryl liked that one and laughed. I laughed too. "But my English teacher, Debbie, her husband is a fisherman out of Cordova, a gillnetter—"

Whatever that means, I thought, still a landlubber in every sense of the word. "—and she said I could make some decent money up in Alaska as a deckhand for the summer. He doesn't have a job for me, but apparently there is a house run by good people with a room I'm renting. I guess all I got to do is walk the docks and ask everyone I see for a job?"

"Oh yes. That is how you're supposed to do it if you don't have a connection," Sheryl insisted. "You're going to have to talk to Bryon's father, I think he knows one guy in particular who is perfect for you."

3

"Really? Thank you!" I celebrated too loudly.

"My dad once hooked a sea lion," Bryon piped up. "It was huge and scary and barked real loud." I made a wow face. Sheryl put a hand on Bryon's head.

"Bryon sure likes to fish with his daddy," Sheryl said. She smiled at her little sprout for a time before looking back at me. Was there a hint of sadness to her eyes? It struck me that perhaps a touch of melancholy is what defines a mother's gaze. I saw it on my own mother's face as she waved goodbye to me at the airport a few hours previous. Dad was there too, although in my experience dads look less melancholy when their sons march off on some kind of journey. My folks were no strangers to this kind of thing having met on a study abroad program to Fiji during their University of Minnesota days. She, the quantitative mind who became a doctor, studied fiddler crabs on the beaches as an aspiring oceanographer. He, the qualitative mind who tapped out of a law career early to write his to-be magnum opus about the Civil War, interviewed tribal elders about Degei the serpent god and served as a navigator on a sailing yacht to Australia.

Overall they seemed more proud than sad to see me go. The only thing for me to do was sling my Coyote 4500 backpack over my shoulder and walk over the tacky but comforting purple and turquoise lines of the PDX carpet. Any Portlander who flew before the 2012 remodel holds that PDX carpet pattern dear to memory. Fans, originally ironic but now genuine, can find t-shirts and socks in the old carpet's likeness.

Now the only way was north and, hopefully, a profitable livelihood at sea.

"I sure hope things work out for you, Norris. You are such a nice young man," Sheryl said softly. I never was one to take a compliment, so I squirmed with Bryon in our seats while she eased back and closed her eyes. I looked out the window. The deep blue of the North Pacific stretched as far as the eye could see, the hide of a great beast I hoped no fisherman would ever master.

"Where are you guys sitting?" I asked Sheryl in the Anchorage airport. We were herded into the much smaller airplane that was to take us to Cordova, a tiny fishing town only accessible by sea or air. There were no roads to Cordova through the jagged teeth of the Chugach Mountains, a barrier so formidable even moose cannot make the journey overland. Humans, always eager to cultivate and slaughter, introduced them to the region for sport and sustenance. Sheryl and I compared tickets. They were sitting elsewhere.

"Bryon, did you see the big polar bear?" I asked. I found the great stuffed animal during our layover, its lips drawn into a snarl and ebony claws bared to strike from behind the glass coffin of a display case. I knew I wouldn't have to worry about polar bears as far south as Prince William Sound, but it did underscore the point. I was on Alaskan soil.

"No!" Bryon pouted and I wished I hadn't brought it up. Sheryl patted him on the head and boarded the plane.

"I'll see you when we land, don't scurry off," Sheryl called over her shoulder. I followed the line onto the craft and approached a gentleman who looked very comfortable at his window seat. I was to be his neighbor as part of a two-person row.

"Pleased to meet you, sir," I said overenthusiastically. Fortunately, unlike some strangers, he didn't look at me like I had a screw loose.

"Howdy," his voice was a rumble from his protruding gut and bullfrog throat. His scruff was heavy but not quite a beard and his plaid shirt gave him a passed-his-prime-lumberjack vibe. His newsboy cap looked proper on his greying head. I shuffled into my aisle seat next to him as smoothly as I could. I knew these first few seconds would dictate whether we flew according to the standard vow of silence or actually conversed like human beings. Whether I sat next to a new friend or a rival eating up my elbow space was halfway in my hands, but only briefly. His howdy? Nearly as enthusiastic as my hello. The choice was clear.

"Going home?" I asked and clipped my seatbelt.

"Nah, nah. But I always spend my summers hunting in the Alaskan or Canadian bush. It's too damn beautiful up here. Name's Bob," he said. We shook hands heartily.

"Pleasure, Bob," I said. "What do ya hunt?" Bob stroked his chin.

"Oh, just about anything that'll fill the freezer with a few trophies I guess," Bob said. The plane took off from the runway without any drama and I stared, mouth agape, at the Alaskan horizon. A handful of white peaks accented an otherwise rolling horizon back home in Oregon. In Alaska, the jagged white teeth of the Earth Mother sheared through the ground in endless rows like a shark's maw. The first charts surely labelled this land Thar be Dragons. A knowing smile crossed Bob's face. "First time to Cordova?"

"First time to Alaska. I just graduated from high school in Oregon and I'm going to Cordova to do some salmon seining. I've never done it before, but I'm renting a room in a house with good people. I hear if I walk up and down the docks and ask everyone I meet for a job, I might get one," I said.

Bob again stroked his chin. "Salmon seining, eh? That is mighty tough work. I've done a lot of the jobs around here, but never did that." He paused. "You can have the window seat," and he was on his feet switching places before I could offer a symbolic objection.

Bob settled into his new seat. "I'll never get tired of the view, but I've seen it a hundred times. Hopefully will a hundred more, hah!"

I pressed my nose up to the glass. We flew further into the shark's maw and my mind wandered to wild things I hoped to see for the first time, creatures like grizzly bears and moose that didn't live in Oregon. One animal preoccupied my thoughts more than the others, the villain of European children's stories and the hero of Native American ones. The one who fears nothing and sings in the night. The one who is wildness incarnate.

"Have you ever seen a wolf?" I asked. "I've always wanted to see one."

Bob nodded. "You bet. I remember this one time we were moose hunting in the Northwest Territories. So here I am with my buddy following a game trail and he has to take a leak, so he pulls over. I says ok, but hurry up, this here's bear country. If you ever go into the woods up here, you got to promise me two things: not alone and with a gun. Understand?" Bob eyed me but didn't wait for my reply. "Anyway, I'm all alone and around the bend comes the biggest wolf I ever did see. The thing seemed bigger than me! Its fur was pitch black and when our eyes met, he froze. I tell ya, if he had taken one more step towards me, I would've blasted the giant beautiful bastard right between the eyes. But here comes my buddy out of the brush and he is all, *holy shit!* with his pants half-on. The wolf just sorta melts away into the forest. It was the craziest thing... glad I didn't have to shoot him."

Neil Armstrong's first lunar words echoed in my head as I left Bob and our flying machine behind. Sheryl and Cap'n Bryon rushed to a lanky, leather-skinned man sporting a silver handlebar mustache and wrapped him in a hug. The man's faded red shirt was tucked into his jeans that were held up with a thin brown belt. A beat-up baseball cap sat on his head. I felt like I had seen him a hundred times beside tackle shops and country roads of contiguous America, places like Newport, Oregon, or Sturgis, North Dakota.

I walked past the Lippincott family, my eyes keen for my English teacher's stepdaughter Kara who was to give me a lift from the airport to town. From what I had gathered, there was only one road through Cordova that connected the town to the airport and ended in the Alaskan bush miles beyond. A road to nowhere. I looked forward to picking Kara's brain, for she was an experienced commercial deckhand and native of Cordova.

"Norris," Sheryl called and I turned. She beckoned me and turned to the man, his arm around her shoulders. "Dale, this is Norris. This young man

7

kept Bryon busy the whole plane ride from Oregon to Anchorage. He is looking for a job as a deckhand around here. You know somebody who can help him out, don't you?" She looked up at Dale with vaguely pleading eyes. He gave me the old once over. Our eyes met silently for a few masculine seconds.

"Well, my buddy Scott Brown Jr. on the *Solstice* will be looking for crew when he gets back in. He is gillnetting right now on the Flats, but he should be in sometime here. You got a pen?" Dale asked. I always did and offered the utensil I liberated from my local credit union. Dale pulled out a sacrificial receipt from his back pocket. He jotted down the number while I did my best to contain myself. I didn't do that great of a job and rubbed my hands together as if starting an invisible fire.

"This is so helpful!" I sputtered. "You'll probably see me out on the docks every day asking everybody I meet for a chance. That's all I need, honest, a chance." Dale grinned and handed me my first lead.

"That's how you got to do it. Someone like you will probably find something," Dale said.

"It was such a pleasure, Norris," Sheryl beamed at me. "Thank you for the nap, I needed it. You happy to be back with your daddy, Bryon?" Little Bryon, out of the airplane, had turned shy. He clutched his toy boat to his chest. My eyes drifted outside to where a young lady maybe a few years older than I leaned against an old pickup truck and scanned the small leaving crowd. I had a hunch I was looking at Kara.

Solstice on the Solstice

An explosion of dog yips followed Kara's knock on the door of Dora Jones' house, my planned base of operations. I stood a few paces back, my Kelty Coyote 4500 pack with my worth slung over one shoulder. Kara gave me an easy, reassuring smile. She was a few inches shorter than me with lightly freckled, rosy cheeks. The chatter during the truck ride from the airport—known locally as 13 Mile—about fishing lingo and Cordovan gossip took the edge off my nerves. I knew a few more things about what was ahead of me fishing-wise and had the gist of a few of the town's characters. Dora was supposed to be one of the good ones.

I stole a glance at the view. Her house was near the top of a rise overlooking downtown Cordova sprawled between us and the harbor. A breakwater bordered the harbor and if all the downtown buildings were smashed together by a divine hand they would've easily fit inside the boundary. I later learned that this region was informally split into two halves, Old Harbor and New Harbor. While technically the same harbor, New Harbor was a large addition to the traditional harbor space, Old Harbor, and the two siblings had different land accesses. The small mountains of Hawkins Island rose across Orca Inlet beyond. From a raven's view, Cordova was a barnacle colony that clung to life at the edge of the sea.

9

The door opened. A smiling woman stuffed herself in the opening to prevent a yapping Jack Russell terrier from running circles between my legs.

"Sophie, no," Dora warned the dog as she hugged Kara warmly and turned to me. Dora's hair was a golden ginger and she stood around six feet tall. "You must be Norris. Welcome to Hawk House." I knew that Dora was the Executive Director of a local environmental advocacy group devoted to preserving the area's salmon spawning habitat. She looked like the outdoorsy, granola-eating, New England attorney turned professional Alaskan environmentalist I expected.

"Good to be here, thank you," I flashed my whites.

"Come in. Darrell is here now, but he is on his way out to fish." Dora beckoned us inside. I took off my trail runners and soaked in the place. The surplus of cushioned armchairs and the warm glow of reading lamps over shelves of books in the living room made for a bookworm's paradise. A bearded man roughly my height but twice my girth in muscle and chest hair reached for his shoes as I put mine aside. He looked like the kind of guy who put on a kilt and threw logs at Highland Games for fun. A quiet wolf-like dog watched us from her bed in the corner.

"You must be Darrell Jones," I grinned and offered my hand. He took it but remained focused on lacing his boots. "It's Darrell Miller. Dora and I are not married," he replied curtly, but not rudely, and finished tying his boots. "That's Zoe," he pointed to the wolf-like dog in the corner. I had a feeling I was partway toward seeing my first wolf when I looked at her.

"Ah," I replied. I wasn't sure what else to say. He turned to Dora and put a hand tenderly on her arm as they looked into each other's eyes. I was instantly made an intruder. Kara beckoned me around a corner and up a flight of stairs. I heard the main door shut behind us.

"You'll be up here in my dad's room, that is until he gets back from fishing the Flats," Kara spoke over her shoulder.

"Your dad is Larry, right?" I asked.

"Yup," Kara hummed and opened one of the white doors lining a small hallway. A modest bed with a night table and window livened up the plainness a little. "Larry, Darrell, Pete, Mel… they are all in the same radio group."

Larry, Mel… what is this, the Stooges?

"Radio group?" I asked.

"Yeah, they all communicate on a 'secret' radio frequency when they're out fishing. You know, to give each other tips and stuff. They even have code words. Some groups go way over the top with it." My left arm was numb under the squeeze of my shouldered pack, so I eased the load to the floor and flexed the arm back to life under my hoodie. "Now, let's see your fishing gear." Kara pointed to the bed. I hefted the pack onto the tired mattress that was more sprung than spring. She blew a strand of dark brown hair from her face as we both leaned forward to see the goods. I pulled out my green work jacket and raingear. Kara handled them eagerly for a few seconds.

"Everyone told me to buy Grundens—" I began.

"These are perfect, brand new and ready to go. But why didn't you get orange?" Kara put my clothes on the bed.

"The orange was a little too… orange?" I shrugged. I hadn't given color much thought at soon-to-be-defunct G.I. Joe's, but the racks of orange rubber raingear looked a little too much like skinned Teletubbies for my taste.

"Well that green—" Kara pointed to my green clothes, "—will be hard to see if you fall overboard into the green water. So, don't do that, ok?"

"I'll do my best," I promised.

"Good," Kara said. She flipped open her cell phone.

"Should I be worried about seasickness?" I asked.

"The waters are generally calmer in Prince William Sound than the open ocean but can still be pretty nasty. The seiners generally work spawning streams and shorelines," Kara replied while texting. "You might want to chew on some ginger candies or something? I don't know really, I've never been seasick. The Flats are totally different and can get really gnarly."

"Roger," I said, not reassured. Kara shut her phone.

"Alright, I've got to meet up with my boyfriend for a little bit. He is coming in on the ferry and I'm his ride from the terminal."

Boyfriend. The word echoed mournfully in my mind. Single, eighteen-year-old males will always inwardly despair when they don't get a fighting chance. Even a one percent chance will motivate a man to monumentally stupid, courageous, inspirational, or insulting action. Sometimes all four simultaneously. I reckon that a feature of the 21st century gent is that he knows what zero percent looks like and graciously accepts the fact, but some beloved scoundrels I've known see good odds where they have no business seeing them. The man's side of things is trickier than I've heard most allow, for the consequences of a simple flirt range from bitter lawsuit to blissful marriage.

"How about I drop you off at the harbor and you start asking around for a deckhand job?" Kara offered. "I'll pick you up at 6:30 in front of the store and we can go to a solstice party BBQ for dinner."

Solstice… that's odd, Scott Brown Jr.'s boat is called the *Solstice*, I mused.

"You know, the solstice slipped my mind," I said.

"Well, it's today. We're grilling up moose burgers. I bet you haven't had one of those before." Kara led me down the stairs.

Moose burgers? My brain had to get used to all the curveballs being thrown at me: unfortunate boyfriends, fateful astronomy, moose burgers, and so on. Dora stood before one of the large living room windows that offered a commanding view of Cordova, the harbor, and beyond. Zoe the wolf-like dog heeled at her side. Kara cleared her throat.

"Norris is getting a tour of the town. I'll bring him back safe in the evening," Kara said. Dora looked away from the ocean.

"Have fun. And truly, welcome. The door is left unlocked, so just let yourself back in. Debbie won't be in town until later in the week, but she is eager to see you. She says you were quite the student body president."

"I haven't seen her since high school graduation two weeks ago. I guess that isn't that long, huh?" I said. Dora's gaze shifted back to the window as we left.

"No, that isn't that long at all," Dora nearly whispered. Her smile faded as I closed the door. I didn't know it then, but it'd be a while since I saw Darrell again. "Gone fishing" has a weightier connotation up there.

I closed my eyes to the hymn of the seagulls and took a deep breath of briny air before I thudded over the wood planks of the raised boardwalk of Old Harbor. Fifty-foot purse seiners and smaller gillnetting boats shifted in their slips under the light breeze like restless horses in racetrack stalls. I nearly skipped to the marina and those steeds of the sea, my rides to adventure and riches. Surly beanie-wearing men tended line or meddled with hydraulic winches. My buffoonish smile was stuck on my face as I bounced my way to the unknown, a lion on the hunt or a lamb to the slaughter.

Place yer bets.

I tromped down the ramp to the docks, a breathtakingly romantic place for a young soul yearning for purpose. A man walked by, his hands sooty from some mechanical chore. He wiped his nose with the back of his wrist and spat in the water. I swooned.

Paradise!

I passed a dozen boats, nervous for my first date on the summer solstice with the *Solstice*. I came upon her after a few minutes. She was a blue hulled, fifty-foot Lombard with twin inboard diesel engines and an aluminum skiff on deck. Kara said she had a reputation for catching fish—a highliner—and Scott Brown Jr. was a skipper who everyone seemed to respect, even if his

13

politics were a little too vocal and deep-red libertarian for some. Considering Scott's peers were keep-the-government-out-of-my-guns-and-pot Alaskans, being labelled as too libertarian certainly said a lot. The cherry on top was that Scott's other boat, a gillnetter, was named the *Leatherneck II*.

I heard Scott Brown Jr. flew the Confederate flag on occasion. The Confederate flag bothered me more than the average white Joe in 2008. Largely thanks to my Abraham Lincoln loving father's spontaneous history seminars (nowhere will you find a prouder First Minnesota Regiment fan) I've always known that the Civil War—or War of Northern Aggression as some still called it in insulated circles—never truly ended in America. In 2008, the conflict played out with the quiet renaming of parks, dubious content of history textbooks reprinted in Texas, and all-too-passionate Gettysburg reenactments of Pickett's Charge. At least it wasn't real bullets and bloody soil. Most of the time. The stars and bars still flew over the South Carolina capital building and rebel statues were commonplace across much of the country.

As a landlubber, I was unsure about boat etiquette, so I loitered alongside the *Solstice* for a few awkward moments. Minutes passed and I began to feel suspicious enough to arouse attention, so I stepped aboard the deck and knocked on the cabin door. A hydraulic arm with a pulley, that I later learned was called the power block, hung overhead; a giant mechanical praying mantis poised to strike from above. A mountain of black webbing and white floats and shiny metal rings was heaped on the flat work deck—the purse seine net.

I gave the door another few taps. Nobody home. The word was that Scott was out fishing on his gillnetter the *Leatherneck II*, so I had no right to be as disappointed as I was. By this time, I knew that fine-mesh gillnets caught fish by tangling up in the gills while the thicker seine nets caught salmon by surrounding them and pulling them in as a bundle. The smaller gillnetters were often one- or two-person operations in Prince William Sound. The larger and more complex seiners usually required a few more deckhands to operate.

Thank you, Kara.

I held my breath and trespassed the cabin, half expecting a loaded shotgun to greet me. Instead, there was a flat-screen TV and the kitchen (galley in boat speak) was fully equipped with a fridge and stovetop oven. These comforts were all reassuring at the cost of a little romance. Every place to sit also doubled up as storage. If houses were like boats, the typical living room couch would be hollowed out to hold a month's ration of non-perishable cans of chili, a toolbox, jugs of motor oil, a collapsible kayak, five rolls of rescue tape, a first aid kit, a flare gun, moldy adult magazines, and a forgotten bag of stale potato chips.

I didn't bring any scratch paper, so I scavenged a napkin from the galley and jotted down something to the effect of:

Me Norris. Me catch fish real good. You Scott Brown Jr. Me work for you?

Cell phone number. Email. Time and date.

I felt pretty good about my masterpiece and propped it up so Scott Brown Jr. couldn't help but see it as he walked in the door. I took a moment to fantasize about what life would be like aboard. Would this place someday be home? I let my hands run along the side of the large dinette table that was complimented with two benches of family-style seating. The important questions were first. What meals would we eat? What laughs would we share? Would they like me? I took my leave after a respectful bow and left the sleeping *Solstice* to slumber. Working aboard such a nice boat seemed a dream more than a goal.

The summer solstice sun was still high in the sky but the hours slipped by all the same. I decided to call it and pound the docks in full force the next day. I left Old Harbor behind on my march to the New Harbor rendezvous with Kara at the grocery store. The sky grew overcast and threatened to rain much like the normal state of things in Oregon. I walked to New Harbor in time to see Bob from the airplane get into a truck with a few of his grizzly peers. The truck bed was loaded with fishing rods and coolers.

"Hey Bob," I waved. Bob looked up. He gave me a big ruddy grin and waved as the truck pulled out. He said something that I couldn't hear over the engine. I never saw Bob again, nor learned whatever farewell wisdom he tried to share.

"Hey there, Norris!" A familiar voice called. I turned and spied Sheryl and the rest of the Lippincotts gathered around an idling truck.

"Hey-oh, Lippincotts!" I greeted and saluted Cap'n Bryon, who was barely visible from where he sat in the back of the truck. Dale nodded and we exchanged a firm handshake before he put an arm around his mamma.

"Any luck?" Sheryl asked. I looked around.

"Well, I was walking around Old Harbor and left a note on the *Solstice*. I'll be pounding the docks hard tomorrow and hope for the best."

"'Bout the best you can do," Dale said. "I'll let Scott know you're here, he usually takes on green horns no problem." He looked over his shoulder. "Time to go." Sheryl looked into my eyes with a surprising, bright-eyed intensity.

"Goodbye and good luck, Norris," she said. I gave her a thumbs up as the truck left. Wouldn't you know it, but I never saw them again either. Small tragedies like the irreverent departure of Bob and the Lippincotts play out a billion times a day in the world. People wiser than me know to never take one of the real people for granted.

I didn't wear a watch like most millennials, so I flipped open my Crazr cell phone for the time. Kara was late. I looked up. The near midnight sun still glowed behind the clouds, drenching the town in surreal, eclipse-like light. Trucks left until only the abandoned ones remained. Old, rusty orphans trapped on the salty side of the Chugach Mountains. There wasn't a living soul in sight. I felt like the only human resident of a town with too many boats.

Eerie.

The screen of my phone blinked at me. The battery was dying. One of the morbid features of my phone was that it vibrated fiercely with its last bit of energy when it ran out of juice. Personally, it was too life-like for my taste, too much like the last struggles of a trout leaping for air at the bottom of a canoe. Small. Helpless. Desperate. Alone.

The screen went black.

I cut my losses and started the walk to Hawk House. It wasn't far, probably half a dozen blocks up the hill. I wondered if Dora was still gazing out her window at the Sound with Zoe the wolf-like dog at her heel. Maybe she was watching Darrell underway to his fishing grounds. I tried not to think of what Kara and her boyfriend were probably doing. The town remained lifeless.

I entered Hawk House and there was no sign of Dora. She must've gone to bed. I tiptoed up the squeaky steps to my room and it was a minor miracle Sophie the Jack Russel didn't sniff me out. I reckoned she was a daytime alarm only.

The day hit me in a wave of exhaustion and I collapsed on my bed. Simple unprocessed thoughts rippled through my brain slime. Thoughts about the cute girls who wrote nice things in my high school yearbook kept my mood light. Musings on my absolute helplessness brought me down. I was completely at the mercy of whatever force it was that pulled my puppet strings. The summer solstice sun glowed behind the window drapes even though it was past eleven. I reached for my journal and squeezed out a few lines of ink: *Right now, I'm alone. I have no job yet, but I think my name is out there. This is truly a WTF adventure.*

Pounding the Docks

Next morning I marched down the hill from Hawk House under a post-solstice sun that fared poorly against the overcast. With the passing of the summer solstice, the light of day steadily lost minutes to the dark of night. But I was in Alaska, technically shy of the midnight sun of the Arctic Circle but not by much relatively speaking. The sun should have reigned supreme, yet the eerie twilight caused by the overcast persisted. A large fluffy puppy watched me from where he was tied up to a porch. I waved at him as I walked past. He smiled and wagged his tail. I resisted the urge to trespass and pet him.

My plan was to snoop around Old Harbor where crewmen took advantage of the morning to work on their seiners. The start of the pink salmon seining season was days away. It was time to mend nets and make sure the engine purred. Fuel up and load supplies. Time, I hoped, to fill that last open crew spot.

The first boat I came upon was a red and black version of the *Solstice* named *Son of Raven*. I approached a man smoking a cigarette on the work deck, his long black hair in a ponytail and his stature short and stocky.

"Ahoy! Permission to come aboard?" I called with a smile. The man smirked in such a way that I instantly learned real fishermen didn't say ahoy.

"Hey der," he offered his hand. We shook.

"My name is Norris. I'm from Oregon and I'm looking for a deckhand job—" He held up his hand.

"I have crew Norris, but it don't madder no how. This is gonna be a lousy season." He took a drag of his cigarette. "Real bad." My smile faltered.

"Really? Why do you say that?" I asked.

"It what everybody thinks. Last year was lousy. The year before was lousy. It's been real bad." He looked out beyond the harbor to the sound. "The oil spill killed all the herring and they ain't coming back. Exxon and their lawyer fuckers are really fucking us." *Son of Raven*'s captain spat in the water. "Fuckers. Best go back home. Gonna be a lousy season."

Is he talking about the *Exxon Valdez* spill? I wondered. I knew the spill happened in 1989, the year I was born and the Soviet Union collapsed. Was there still a court case? Herring? I made a mental note to look into it. I handed him a piece of torn paper from my journal with contact info scribbled on. Poor man's business cards.

"Well, thanks for the tip. If you hear about anything opening up, let me know," I said. He nodded and we split ways. I approached the next seiner, a good-sized looker called the *Edmond W*. An older man with a frizz of white hair emerged from the cabin as I came along her side.

"Ahoy!" I greeted him. He turned about with a bemused chortle. I continued to fall out-of-love with the word ahoy.

"How do you do," he replied courteously with a refined British accent that caught me off-guard.

"My name is Norris. I'm from Oregon and I'm looking for a deckhand job on a seiner for the season. Are you looking for crew?"

"Ah," the man brightened and looked over my shoulder.

"You are?" I blurted.

"Oh, um, sorry, no. I'm all set for crew," the man said as he crossed his arms. I turned around to see two young men about my age, maybe a year or two younger, walk toward us with lazy saunters. "I'm Charles. Charles Wood," Charles smiled and we shook, he aboard and I on the dock. "Those two are my son's crew and were supposed to be here an hour ago. My son's name is Edmond. He is the hired skipper on this boat right here."

Charles beckoned to the seiner in the adjacent slip. *Rikki-Tikki-T* was written on her dark blue hull. She was a few feet shorter than the *Edmond W*, a forty-seven-foot Delta. The two young men reached us and I could feel them size me up. I was the new dog in the park.

"James! Hunter!" Charles got their attention. "Do either of you know of any deckhand jobs? Norris here is from Oregon and pounding the docks." James was about my size with the same shaggy brown hair while Hunter stood about six-foot and sported a tight buzz cut. We shook hands.

"Yeah bro, Scott's looking for crew on the *Solstice*," James said.

"I left a note on his boat. He's fishing the Flats, right?" I said. James nodded.

"Yo, I'll call him for you," James said. He flipped open his phone, pushed a button, and put the device to his ear in one smooth motion. Hunter rolled his eyes.

"You got Scott on speed dial? Dude, that's too much. Just suck his dick already," Hunter teased and bobbed around a slap from James' free hand. Hunter looked at me with a grin and pointed at James. "Seriously, this guy is nuts for Scott."

"The guy is a fucking legend, alright?" James hissed before he answered a voicemail. "Yo Scott, I found you a crewmember man. Get back to me. When you're back, maybe we can go shooting—"

"A date," Hunter whispered loudly and dodged another slap. The clouds continued to strangle the sun. Cold misty rain began to drizzle. Charles shook his head, a little more fed up with the world. I handed him my contact info and he took it.

"I'll let you know if I hear anything," Charles said and re-entered his cabin. James clasped his cell shut.

"I appreciate it, man," I said to James. We exchanged a sideways high five with a satisfying slap. Nailed it.

"Legit dude," James said. "We gotta bounce, catch you on the flip side."

"Totally, brah," I said. The bro aftertaste in my mouth was a small price to pay for a few friendly faces. Hunter and I exchanged manly nods and they boarded the *Rikki-Tikki-T*. I felt a bit better. At least they didn't tell me to go home.

I walked past one of the smallest seiners of the fleet, a vintage looking vessel with brown and red trimmings. The seine net wasn't aboard yet and the deck needed a good clean. Nobody was aboard getting her ready. A pirate flag hung limp over the entrance to the cabin.

The Sil-Ver-Fish, *eh? Little party boat...*

I pressed on, less interested in a good time than a good job. A clean seiner with a red and grey hull enticed me, so I hopped aboard and knocked on the cabin door. The name *Alcor* graced her bow. The door opened and an old man with a faded ball cap and friendly wrinkled forehead appeared. He looked like the kind of grandpa anybody would be lucky to grow up with.

"Howdy," he said warmly. "What can I do for you?"

"My name is Norris. I'm from Oregon and I'm looking for a deckhand job on a salmon seiner—"

"Joe, who's there?" A woman's voice came from the back of the cabin. Joe turned.

"It's a kid from Oregon looking for a deckhand job. His name is Norris."

"Invite him in out of the rain," the lady insisted. Joe's face creased into a warm smile that was shy a few teeth.

"Get on in here Norris and have a seat," Joe said. I was ushered to a comfortable table inside. Pictures of family hung on the walls and a tired, but clean, tablecloth lay over the table. The cabin smelled like cinnamon apple tea bags and baking cookies. The rain pitter-pattered against the windows in a lullaby as the woman rose to her feet. Somebody could've told me I was in a gingerbread house and I would've believed him.

"My name is Connie," she beamed and we shook hands. "Sit. I'll make you some hot cocoa."

"I—" I began, but Connie was already off to the galley with a kettle in-hand and back with a platter of chocolate chip cookies. "—wow, thanks," I stared at the platter. Joe took a cookie. I grabbed mine after he took his first bite.

"So, young fella, you're looking to be crew?" Joe asked.

"Yes sir," I swallowed. "Do you have your crew for the season?"

"I don't," Joe replied. My heart soared. "But I don't think I'll be going out this season." Connie joined us and passed me a steaming mug of hot cocoa. "I'm still thinking about it, but it's getting a little late for that. Most guys are already starting to head out."

"Thank you," I smiled at Connie and let the mug cool. She sat next to Joe, her posture perfect and her silver hair neat. "Are you not going out because this season is supposed to be lousy?" I asked. Joe chuckled.

"You've heard about that, huh? Yeah, there's that… also, this old body ain't what it used to be." Joe gave Connie a lopsided grin. She held his hand on the table and their fingers intertwined. It was about the gentlest scene I ever saw. Old Joe sighed, content. "Oregon, huh?"

I stayed with Joe and Connie on the *Alcor* for a while. Half an hour? An hour? Two? All day? Time behaves strangely sometimes. They wanted to hear about my life, and I mostly told them about high school and how awesome my little sister was. My sister and I hung out with the orangutans the most at the zoo and had a favorite conveyor belt sushi place. The main takeaway from being student body president was that it was a worthwhile experience but probably the pinnacle of my political career. I told them about my mom, a women's and children's doctor and medical researcher who they might've heard on National Public Radio talk about breast cancer, and my dad, a burnt-out lawyer turned greatest living unpublished Civil War historian. I didn't think I was all that interesting, but they weren't after wild stories and wanted to hear every detail. I had to rally all my willpower to decline a second hot cocoa and dismiss myself. I left my contact info and, despite Connie's gentle objections, returned to the fog and Cordovan drizzle.

I stopped by a few more seine boats but they were empty. Or maybe they didn't want to talk to me. Who knew. Who cared. My stomach began to growl. Connie's cookies had been my only lunch. I took my rebelling gut as a sign that I gave Old Harbor a good enough shake for the day. I walked up the hill and past the large fluffy puppy to Hawk House. Sophie went ballistic while I warmed up at the doorway. Dora was curled up on a couch, probably recently returned from work.

"Fine weather here in Cordova," I joked, soaked.

"Best get used to it," Dora smiled. "Hey, you don't have any plans tonight, do you?" I shook my head. "Want to go to a seafood potluck? One of my friends has a visiting marine biologist friend who has been taking wildlife photography in the Prince William Sound. He is going to give us a slideshow and talk about what he found. Are you into that kind of thing?"

I eased onto the carpeted living room floor of Dora's friend among the dozen or so other guests. We gazed at the glowing slideshow of biologist and amateur photographer Matt in the pleased, vacant way campers gaze into a bonfire. The seafood offerings from the guests were spread upon a foldable table positioned against the far wall: local freshly shucked oysters on half shells with lemon slice compliments, whole spotted prawns with horseradish-rich cocktail sauce made from scratch, a pile of snow crab legs the size of a Thanksgiving turkey, giant slabs of flakey, perfectly cooked Chinook salmon, great steaks of buttery halibut, and literal buckets of mussels and clams. The seafood faire of this potluck was fit for New York bankers to pay $200 for, but these were delicacies that are common in a Cordovan freezer or backyard. I was on my third plate of crab and half oysters in a matter of minutes.

Matt's show thus far featured many of the charismatic local megafauna, including breaching humpback whales, grizzly bear families fishing at river mouths, and pods of orcas. He looked as one imagines a marine biologist whose artistic outlet is photography to look; middle aged and silver foxy with square-framed glasses and a trim physique under a water-wicking quasi-safari button up shirt and cargo pants.

"And here," Matt clicked a button. The image on the projector shifted from the black dorsal fins of killer whales to a hole in the sand of a nearby beach. Ooze blacker than the orcas puddled.

"To the west of Cordova on Smith Island, we can see crude oil from the *Exxon Valdez* disaster of 1989 is still present in the sediments. I'm sure most of you here are familiar with the collapse of the herring fishery after the oil spill. Well, I'm sorry to say recent studies indicate that the herring numbers won't recover anytime in the near future, if ever."

The words of the *Son of Raven* captain echoed in my memory: *The oil spill killed all the herring and they ain't coming back. Exxon and their lawyer fuckers are really fucking us.*

I realized I was looking at photographic evidence of the man's complaints. More images of black ooze on the beach flipped past. Digital scans of faded pictures from the seventies flashed by of grinning fishermen and seines full to bursting with herring, a memory from Cordova's glory days. The show ended with a blank slide and a quiet, humbled audience. I tried to focus on small talk as the party wound down, but black puddles of oil gunked the focus of my thoughts. Whatever the future held, I wouldn't be chasing herring.

Three Captains

The week inched by as a slow montage, the music of which was performed by a sleepy cellist prodded by an anxious conductor. Not being an early riser but forever envious of them, I typically awoke fairly late in the morning to scuttle down the hill from Hawk House. As part of the ritual, I passed the large fluffy puppy and adjusted course to either Old or New Harbor. I checked up on the few captains who seemed on-the-fence and the many who already told me no.

Joe and Connie on the *Alcor* always invited me in when they saw me walk by, but I got in the habit of declining. I had a job to find and I worried I'd go in and not leave all day. Once Joe insisted on giving me a ride between Old and New Harbor to spare me the Cordova drizzle. I was incapable of refusal. He told me of his final decision not to fish. I spent some of my dwindling savings on salty black licorice, my favorite candy, to avert an unbearably blue mood. Fishing with kindly old Joe and Connie seemed like the ideal situation.

After three days of walking and getting the boot from most of the sea salts in town, I decided to diversify my tactics. I hopped on Dora's computer and created a poster that was to be the center of a public relations blitz. I had access to a limited number of my pictures via my fledgling Facebook page, a recent addition to my and most of my friends' lives. I was more of a

LiveJournal sort of guy, but such were the times. I found a flattering picture of me in a farmer John wetsuit from a rafting trip. A white bandana held back a mane of flowing high-school era hair. My jaw was tightened into a serious expression as I gazed off-frame to a horizon of opportunity. The angle of the shot was taken from below, and all five feet, nine and three-quarter inches of me towered like a giant vision of Manifest Destiny meets Rambo. Stubs for the number to Hawk House hung at the bottom.

I kept my message simple: NEED CREW? HIRE NORRIS! *I'm an eighteen-year-old Oregonian who works hard and doesn't cause trouble. I learn quickly and I'll help you catch your fish.*

I plucked a few of the phone number stubs from each poster to create the impression of desirability and posted them everywhere I could manage along the main drag in town: the store, Old Harbor, New Harbor, the Reluctant Fisherman Inn, the harbormaster's office, the ferry terminal, telephone poles, trees, and the list goes on. I made a point to always carry a few of the fliers to hand out to potentially helpful acquaintances when I was out and about. Dora put one poster in the window of her non-profit and my likeness stood alongside the many anti-Exxon signs posted by other small businesses. *Exxon Made $, We Paid $* and *No Herring, No Justice* come to mind.

Through my process of casual questioning and armed with the benefit of hindsight, I learned that the Supreme Court was on the verge of handing down a decision on the *Exxon Shipping Co. v. Baker* case after nearly twenty years of litigation. From what I could piece together, an Anchorage-based federal jury in 1994 awarded around 32,000 commercial fisherfolk, business owners, etc. $287 million in compensatory damages and $5 billion in punitive damages. While Exxon paid the compensatory damages, they appealed the punitive damages. After the most epic saga of Alaska jurisprudence ever, June 2008 saw the Supreme Court cap the punitive damage figure at $507.5 million—roughly one tenth the original ruling.

The wound from 1989 was still freshly cut in Cordova and nobody seemed optimistic as the final agonizing scene of the tragedy was nigh. I was learning that a cultural identity is not purely a matter of dollars and cents, and sometimes no amount of money can replace an entire livelihood or revive the wounded spirit of a people. I highly recommend the book *The Spill: Personal Stories from the Exxon Valdez Disaster* by Sharon Bushell and Stan Jones (2009) for those looking for firsthand accounts and excellent journalism on the topic.

When the dust from the settlement finally cleared, I investigated the topic a bit further. I heard through the grapevine in Cordova that those who lost millions were awarded thousands. Those who lost thousands received hundreds—sometimes nothing. Later that year *The Seattle Times* published an interview with a fisherman who was twenty-eight/nine and owned three herring boats at the time of the spill. He was initially ruled $2.5 million for the approximately twenty years of lost profits and destruction of his entire livelihood but was ultimately awarded about $180,000 total. To put that into perspective, that allotment was probably not enough to cover the costs for one year's worth of herring fishing for his boats. The man, Mike Webber, was quoted as calling the case "an open sore" on the community.

The collective cheer of "Justice is served. Hip hip, hurrah!" from my fellow citizens of this great land was so deafening that it couldn't be heard.

One place in town that became a familiar safe house for me was the local pet store owned by a woman named Osa Schultz and her husband. I decided to make my introduction to Osa after word got around that we were graduates from the same high school. Osa's son was set to follow our steps in the coming year. Walking Sophie the Jack Russell had somehow become one of my daily Hawk House duties, and one inglorious weekday I figured a visit to the pet store was appropriate. I found Osa outside the pet store with a needle of mending twine and a gill net. Strands of silver colored her ash brown hair and she looked at me with bright brown eyes. She wore faded work jeans and a puffy green thermal jacket.

"Norris?" She asked. Sophie yipped and zigzagged against her leash in an attempt to molest the poor woman.

"Yup. Osa?" We shook hands. Osa tried to pet Sophie. The terrier was too excitable, so Osa sat on a wood crate out of range.

"Nice to meet you," Osa grinned as she flipped open a large knife. I stiffened and Sophie stopped yapping. Osa started to cut the gill net web with the nonchalance of a professional and carried on the conversation. "I'm from Portland too. Funny how a small Alaskan fishing town sucks you in, isn't it?"

"Yeah, what are the odds? A small town like this and a small school like ours. And I understand your son is going to carry on the tradition." We chatted for a good while and the topic switched to that of the oil spill. Osa was to testify in front of Congress on behalf of the Cordovan community. We bantered for a time and ceased to be strangers. I wished her luck with her trip to D.C. and left the pet store thoroughly impressed.

The excitable Sophie proved to be an impossible companion. I only brought her with me once to pound the docks and quickly resolved to tie her up so I could introduce myself to potential employers without subjecting them to Sophie's ankle nips. But she somehow managed to be an even greater annoyance when tied up and ran in circles while making piteous howls after I took three steps from her. I sighed and untangled her from the leash. About the only place I could take her and maintain a level of peace was up Ski Hill, a scenic trail that overlooked the whole bay. The oldest single seat ski lift in America wound down its slope, a historic landmark I didn't expect to see in little Cordova.

The excitement of the first few days faded as the sleepy cellist continued to play. The sun rarely showed itself in Cordova through the rain and my daily ritual of hiking several urban miles and being unwanted by every skipper I met wore me down. I awoke in the mornings to a mental molasses and it didn't help that I was repeatedly told the season was to be lousy and Exxon was fucking us by every other person I encountered. I even contemplated a $15 an hour carpentry job the harbormaster strongly recommended I take. He went on to share a few horror stories of green deckhands who worked without signing a contract and got no pay at the end of the season from their duplicitous captains. I left him my poor man's business card and one of my posters to hang.

I dug into Hawk House's book collection during the evenings. Dora had my kind of taste, tales of explorers, adventure, and nature. I polished off a biography about President Roosevelt's disastrous Amazon expedition, *The*

River of Doubt by Candice Millard, and shook my head at the Americans' poor choice of riverboats. I cruised through an account of Vitus Bering's expedition to Alaska, *Where the Sea Breaks Its Back* by Corey Ford, and sadly contemplated the extinction of the Stellar Sea Cow. The thirty-foot manatees were all devoured by shipwrecked Russians shortly after their discovery. Accounts describe how after one sea cow was felled, the sea cows for miles around would gather around their fallen comrade and keen. The mourning ritual proved to be their downfall, for they were slaughtered en masse. Not one was even spared as a scientific specimen. I read *Ordinary Wolves* by Seth Kantner and was shocked by the wasteful hunting practices and bloodlust of the new generation of native Alaskans. I also continued to daydream of an encounter with a wolf. Somewhere out there, the wolf I was to meet howled and killed and ran with the pack. Every book I read was oddly reassuring, and I would go to bed inspired by the courage of those who struggled in wild environs far from the familiar.

Joe and Connie weren't aboard the *Alcor* one day. I'd never see them again, a theme of post-high school life that saddened me about as much as the weather and my unemployment. Every once in a while, a nice skipper knew a skipper who knew a skipper and I'd walk away with a number and an encouraging word or two. I'd return the next day and the nice guy's slip would be empty. Gonzo. Something in me desired closure, a "keep the chin up, kid," at the very least, but a final genuine moment was just too much to ask. It bugged me that I never knew when to say goodbye to the people I met. The great net of the universe can be a real bitch. My journal took on a vaguely defeated tone and I consoled myself with phrases like, *well, at least I got a little adventure in.*

A highlight of the day was usually having dinner with Dora, for she was a kind and intellectual soul who liked to talk about books and world events. We saw the movie *Tasogare Seibei*, aka *The Twilight Samurai*, one evening.

Iguchi Seibei, the protagonist, was a samurai turned bureaucrat who lost the ability to fight without regard for his life after experiencing the joy of raising his two daughters. Naturally, he is forced to fight again. For some reason it made me think of Darrell. He was still at sea. I often caught Dora looking out over the water.

To my surprise, I was sought after by exactly three captains on the one-week anniversary of my arrival to Cordova.

I'll never know why they all acted on the same day. Maybe it was the last call for the season. The first opener of the Valdez pink salmon run was fast approaching. Or maybe it was coincidence, or fate if coincidence is a farce. Whatever the cause, I found myself in the passenger seat of a truck parked outside of Hawk House.

Captain Rick of the seiner *Sharon* drove up the hill to check me out. He sported a modest mop of silver hair paired with a Van Dyke beard and wore a tan Carhart jacket over a black tee shirt. The man had a slight build, but it was hard to size him up properly inside the truck. A blonde boy roughly my age sat in the back, his blue eyes hard and his mouth quick to leer.

"Hey, Captain Rick," I grinned and extended my hand. Rick squeezed it too tightly without meeting my gaze.

"Here's the deal. I have someone else for the job, but he is green and I'm not sure how tough he is. You heard of the term screamer?" I shook my head. "It means a skipper who lights a fucking fire under your ass. It's a skipper that gets things fucking done and catches some fucking fish. Got it? If you work for me, you are going to do whatever I say, when I say, and not cry or quit like a little bitch."

Now Rick looked me in the eyes. I met Rick's gaze. The blonde boy smirked in brazen superiority. I started to get an unsettling Aryan Youth vibe from blondie. My friendly smile didn't falter. Perhaps it was frozen there.

"Are you tough enough?" Rick asked.

"I can take anything you can dish out," I said. Too cocky? Too cheerful? I'll never know, men have strange standards. One guy may think you're great because you're funny. Another might think you're a moron cause you're always cracking jokes. One guy could value your opinion because you're smart. Another could beat you up because you're a smartass. The truck idled quietly. The Cordova drizzle tapped on the windshield.

"I'll call you in a few hours with my decision," Rick said and waved me out of his car.

Dismissed.

"Thank you for your time and I promise you, if I'm hired, I'll catch a lot of fish," I stammered. "It was nice meeting you." Rick wasn't listening and Blondie wasn't smiling. I stepped out of the truck slightly dazed. The truck peeled away over gravel as I reentered Hawk House. Did that really happen? Sophie's tireless barking filled my ears. Zoe the wolf-like dog spared me a disinterested glance from her corner.

"How'd it go?" Dora clapped her hands together, eyes wide with hope. *Get this guy out of my house already*, she may have thought. I shrugged.

"I'm not sure, but I'll know in a few hours. Say, do you know what a screamer is?" I asked.

"That's what they call a skipper who yells a lot at his crew," Dora nodded. "Why?"

"No reason." I bid her good luck at work. I camped out at Hawk House by the phone and the rainy window to polish off the *Sand County Almanac*. I pondered Aldo Leopold's idea to move the Rim Road of the Grand Canyon away from the very edge. I liked the idea of hordes of overweight families earning their view with a short hike through the desert to get an honest taste of the place. I'd never been to the Grand Canyon, an arid wonderland so opposite from perpetually soaked Cordova. It sounded nice. The phone sat in cruel silence as the clock on the wall ticked past the hour before finally ringing. I sprinted across the room and picked it up.

"Hello?"

"Norris," said Captain Rick.

"Rick—" I began.

"Yeah, look, I'm going with the other guy," he said.

"Alright—" I swallowed. "I—"

"Yup, see ya. Bye."

Rick hung up. Charming fellow.

I was about to retreat into the sanctuary of Aldo Leopold and the last of my salty black licorice when the phone rang again. I paused and turned around. This call was probably for Dora. Or maybe it was Dora, wondering if I was getting out of her house yet. I owed her $100 for my first week, a sizeable piece of cheddar off my modest cheese wheel. I answered.

"Is this Norris?" A man asked in a masculine baritone.

"Yep, who is this?" I asked.

"This is Scott Brown Jr." I restrained an unseemly gasp. *The* Scott Brown Jr. was speaking to *me*.

"Captain of the *Solstice*? You're back from The Flats."

"Yup, it's time to go seining. I got your note and people have been recommending you. You must be pretty persistent," said Scott.

"Yes, sir. I am definitely that."

I held my breath.

"How about you come on down to the *Solstice*. If this works out, we leave tomorrow for the Valdez run," he said. I nearly choked.

"We?"

"Yeah. Can you get down here soon?"

"Yes, sir," I replied and the conversation ended. I spun around to where Zoe napped in the corner of the living room. Sophie snapped to attention.

"Holy crap, you guys." Zoe opened an eye. "I'm a fisherman!" Zoe went back to sleep while I jigged in celebration with a yipping Sophie and fetched my raincoat.

I could've walked from Hawk House to the *Solstice* blindfolded by then and saluted the large fluffy puppy as I skipped to Old Harbor. The *Solstice*'s cabin door was ajar so I let myself in. A scrawny boy of around ten or twelve years sat at the table where he dangled a string over a lighter. His feathered hair was a tawny brown. He was so focused on the flame he didn't notice me. Tendrils of foul-smelling smoke rose from the melting string and I scrunched my nose.

Captain Scott Brown Jr. stood in the middle of the cabin and turned about when I entered. He was a couple inches taller than me with a shaved head and dense build. His eyes were ice blue and I felt like he knew what I was made of the second our gazes met. Scott's shaven head was smooth and his face ruddy, his demeanor confident and calm. I couldn't imagine a scenario that would faze him. The boy's gaze shifted to me for a second before he continued his work with the lighter.

"Hello Captain Scott Brown Jr., I'm Norris. You called me."

We shook hands.

"Sure did. You can call me Scott."

"Yes sir, Captain Scott Brown—" I stopped.

Scott's blue eyes put me under a floodlight before he sniffed the air and turned to the boy.

"Bud, that smells nasty. Can you take that outside?" Scott asked. The boy, intent on his task, kept burning. "Anthony," Scott barked in a level voice. The boy snapped out of it and pouted at his father.

"It doesn't smell that bad," Anthony protested. Scott drilled Anthony with a flat expression that his son squirmed under. The boy finally shot to his feet and left with an overly dramatic *ugh*. He slammed the cabin door shut behind me.

"Thanks, bud," Scott called and turned his attention back to me. "Do you have any fishing experience?" I shrugged.

"I've fished with a pole," I offered.

"Can you cook?" Scott asked.

I shrugged again.

"I can cook some. I'm a fast learner and as eager and determined as anybody you're likely to find."

Scott nodded.

"Learning quick is good. Well, I always pay my deckhands a 10% share. Some boats will start a new guy out at 8%, but that never made sense to me. Greenhorns are doing the same work as the rest of us. The others of this year's crew aren't that experienced either. You'll pick things up and after a bit be a pro. Just always be at the boat when you're supposed to and don't quit on me."

He shifted. I took a break from eye contact. It was a bit exhausting.

"Two seasons ago, one of my crew quit midseason cause he missed his mom. He started crying in the middle of a set and insisted that we drop him off. We did and didn't let him back on when he wanted to get back in the game. Understood? Be on time or I'll leave you behind. Quit and you're dead to me. Learn fast like you say you do and be as determined as you've been on the docks and we'll have a great season. People speak pretty highly of you."

His voice was clear and all-American deep, a melodious, no-nonsense growl with few fluctuations. I was pretty convinced guys like him stormed Omaha Beach in Normandy a few generations ago. I nodded and clenched my fist.

"I won't let you down," I vowed.

"Good," Scott replied. The cabin door opened and I turned. A lanky boy a year or two younger than me entered. He wore black skinny jeans and a purple beanie over long, straight, ebony hair. He tucked a skateboard under his arm. Scott greeted him.

"So, you're Barney Bishop's son?" The boy's eyes darted to me and back to Scott. I guessed he was Athabascan with skin a few shades darker than mine and vaguely Asiatic facial features.

"Yup," he replied.

"I'm Norris," I offered my hand and we shook. His face relaxed a bit and a smile almost broke.

"Al," he said. We both turned back to Scott.

"How's Barney doing?" Scott asked.

"Out fishing already on the *Carmen Lilly*," Al puffed out his chest, proud. Scott smirked. If Scott was the chuckle type he would've.

"Already? Hell of a guy," said Scott.

"What happened?" I asked. Al dug into his pocket and took out one of those new first-generation iPhones people were going nuts over. I wasn't too keen on them. Obviously a fad.

"Dude, it's super gnarly," Al showed me a picture. It was an overview shot of a middle-aged man's balding head. A red gash interlaced with fresh stiches tore over the skull's dome. "Fishing accident. My dad is a badass."

"Woah," I laughed nervously. I cringed inwardly. Scott shook his head in a sort of amused salute of respect.

"Well, welcome Al. I was telling Norris that deckhands get 10% shares. You've been fishing a bit, right?" Al, nodded.

"Yeah, I was on the *Blue Dog* for a bit, but they aren't fishing anymore. Engine problems and they kept saying the season is going to be lousy," said Al. Scott smirked.

"Quitters. More fish for us then. Be here tomorrow at noon to load up food and move in. Then we leave. Understood?" Scott said. Al and I nodded before we left the cabin and stepped off the deck. Anthony glanced at us from where he held his burning lighter.

"Nyah nyah!" Anthony jeered at us as we walked away. "Niggas!" If there's one word that makes a Portland, Oregon-raised liberal snowflake like me bristle, it's that one.

"What the fuck?" Al mumbled as Anthony darted back into the cabin. I shrugged.

"You go to school around here?" I ventured.

"Yeah, it's bullshit. I failed fucking chemistry so I have to make that up. Gay-ass shit, man," Al steamed. Back then, gay was commonly interchangeable with "sucks" or "lame." Don't ask me how that became a thing. I felt a pang of sympathy for the word gay and its journey from happy to homosexual to lame.

"Quite," I agreed. "What's it like living here?"

"It's ok, but the towns around here are pretty boring. Cordova doesn't have a skate park, but Valdez does. I guess when there's snow we've got some wicked snowboarding. A lot of my family lives on tribal land in Tatitlek, but everybody there is old and fat and boring."

I was pretty sure Allen Bishop was the kind of kid who showed up late to school with a fresh cast on his wrist and drew penises under his desk at the back of the class. I liked him and was glad he had at least a little experience from his family and working on the *Blue Dog*. Al hopped on his board and we split ways. I jogged up the hill to Hawk House and blew the large fluffy puppy a kiss through the haze of perpetual Alaskan summer twilight.

"I did it, world!" I wanted to yell.

I threw open the door of Hawk House with a crash and Sophie exploded in her kennel. I let her out and she ran circles around the house, egged on by my mania. I froze at the ring of the house phone and picked up the receiver.

"Hello? This is Hawk House," I said.

"Yo. Is there a guy named Norris there?" A young man's voice asked.

"Yup, this is Norris. How may I help you?"

"Dude! I'm Johnny, the skipper of the *Sil-Ver-Fish*. Your posters are epic awesome! I need crew and I want to hire you." My eyelashes fluttered as I remembered the little party boat with the pirate flag that needed a good scrub. Well, ain't I suddenly the cutest belle at the ball?

"You're a little too late. Scott Brown Jr. just hired me to work on the *Solstice*. I'm spoken for, sorry," I said. *It's not you, it's me. We're just in different phases of life now and I don't want to hold you back, dahling.*

"Aww, really? Well, thanks man and good luck. I'll probably see you out there. For real, sick posters, man," said Johnny.

"Thanks, Johnny. See you out there."

The Job

The sun visited Cordova for a change when I walked up Ski Hill a final time before my departure on the *Solstice*. Debbie, my high school English teacher who tipped me off about this whole Alaska thing, joined me. She arrived in town the previous night with her husband Larry and their labradoodle, Lulu, who joined the pack with Sophie and Zoe. Larry worked as an artisan potter in the off-season and had lived several formative years in Finland learning the craft. He was a very friendly fellow with the silver walrus mustache of a Polish hussar. Upon meeting him, Larry was launched into contention for most interesting man I'd met in Alaska thus far.

Another one of the radio group gillnetters joined us at Hawk House that night, a soft-spoken middle-aged fellow named Pete who seemed to have the dirt on everyone. Apparently, Darrell was doing fine and would be home soon after making some decent coin gillnetting. Jazz music played as the lights dimmed and glasses of red wine emptied. Debbie and Larry recalled the days when they were both young academics at the University of Minnesota in the sixties. I tried to picture a groovy, beret-wearing Debbie with a copy of Yates' *Revolutionary Road* under her arm. During those days, edgy Larry smuggled hashish across the Turkish border during his extensive travels. I loved them for it. I secretly dubbed the group the Hawk House Intellectuals and absorbed what they said like a sponge.

Debbie set a strong pace through the brush on our walk. All three dogs were with us: Sophie, Zoe, and Lulu. Debbie was rereading *War and Peace* and I yearned to borrow it for my fishing trip. As hard as I might, I cannot recall the details of our conversation. We no doubt made great strides in understanding the human condition.

I arrived a bit early to the *Solstice* to find Scott Brown Jr., Al, and an unfamiliar high school kid assembled around Scott's pick-up truck near Old Harbor. I had a hunch the new face belonged to Noah Feingold, our skiffman.

"Hey, Al," I grinned. He smiled back.

"Hey man," Al said. I turned to the new guy.

"You must be Noah? I'm Norris." Noah had the rangy look of a cross-country runner and dark, greasy locks. Scant black bristles began a teenage mustache.

"Yeah yeah, nice to meet you," Noah spoke in a quick mumble and we shook hands. He seemed like a good, if not a little jittery, fellow. I liked him. Scott nodded in approval.

"You guys load up the food. Noah, we're going to practice driving the skiff with my dad and his skiffman, Lance," said Scott. The two of them left Al and me to load up boxes of iced tea tallboys, pounds of moose burger, hundreds of cans of home-smoked salmon, frozen halibut steaks, hamburger helper pasta, Doritos, Cheetos, pop tarts, sacks of potatoes, trail mix, and whatever else a Doomsday prepper with unhealthy eating habits could desire. We watched Noah pilot the skiff while we loaded the goods. He drove away from Scott Brown Sr.'s seiner, the *Mantis*, with Scott Brown Jr. and Lance the seasoned skiffman. A jowly old duffer emerged from the cabin to yell words that sounded more like growls than human speech.

"Lance! What der fuck yer doing? There ain't fuel in dert thing!"

"That's Scott Brown Senior," Al said. "He is the crankiest old man in town."

"Scott's dad, eh? Scott doesn't seem to be like that," I half whispered.

"Yeah," Al said. "Here's hoping."

"We're good, I filled it up earlier," Lance yelled back. Senior shook his head and muttered to himself as he walked back to the cabin. Noah looked a little nervous at the helm, but the skiff cruised about the harbor at low speeds just fine.

"Do you know if Noah has any experience?" I asked and handed Al a two-box stack of canned salmon. I grabbed another and marched to the *Solstice*.

"I think he said he worked on a tender for a few months. His family is a fishing family too," said Al.

"That's right, his dad is in the same radio group as the people who live in the house I've been staying in," I said. I was somewhat reassured that at least my fellow crewmates seemed to know what they were doing, even if I didn't.

Thud!

We both cringed and turned. Noah had bumped the skiff into a floating dock. Senior emerged from the cabin again.

"What der hell are yer doing?!" Senior roared.

Preparation took all day, but the *Solstice* motored out of Cordova Harbor on June 30 for Valdez. We passed the giant wood pilings of a local cannery and a white curtain of a thousand seagulls parted for our passage. I could've plucked one from the sky from where I stood on deck. The *Solstice* steamed out of Orca Inlet to enter the fjord cathedral of Prince William Sound. A cluster of sea otters watched us pass from their knotted kelp bed. The Alaskan summer sun colored the waves gold. Life was uncompromising perfection in that way only boats make possible.

"Norris!" Scott called me up to the wheelhouse. I marched across the deck to the ladder and was at his side in a few seconds. "Whales at ten o'clock. Thought you might be interested." I scanned the water through the windshield and was rewarded with broad grey backs and geysers of breath. I pegged them for humpbacks.

"Oh wow!" I gasped. Scott looked amused. "This is all probably standard for you, huh?"

"Yup," Scott said neutrally, his eyes hidden behind dark sunglasses. My eyes wandered to the bow where black and white Dall's porpoises played in our wake. "Just another day in God's country." I ooh'ed and ahh'ed at his side until I felt obnoxious and excused myself to the cabin.

"Let me know if you see anything else. I love this stuff," I said.

"Will do," Scott said as I closed the floor hatch that fed directly into the cabin. I planted my feet and took in the *Solstice*'s interior. It was only days ago that I entered for the first time, fresh off the airplane and with an eager bounce in my stride. To actually work aboard seemed about as likely as flying off on the *USS Enterprise*. Survivor's *Eye of the Tiger* was blasting from somewhere.

"Out of the way!" Little Anthony yelled at me. He brandished a Wii Guitar Hero controller in my face.

"Huh?" I turned around. I was standing in front of the TV. "Ooops." I moved and Anthony's fingers attacked the neck of the plastic thing. Al was beside Anthony, hungry for a turn.

"You should've gone for easy, man," Al goaded.

"Shut it, nigga!" Anthony plugged away. I blinked. Feisty Anthony was no charming Cap'n Bryon.

"Use star power," Al prompted. "You're going down, dude." Anthony jerked the guitar controller up and the screen illuminated blue. Noah reclined around the table with an iced tea tallboy and a bag of Doritos to watch. I fished some beef jerky out of one of the food cubbies, a settee in sailor speak, and joined him. We exchanged contented nods and zoned out looking at the Guitar Hero screen. Anthony barely got through his song.

"Take that nigga!" Anthony jeered at Al.

"Good job you little shit. My turn," Al took control of the guitar and scrolled through the song list. Noah and I left Al to impress Anthony and entered the v-berth to claim our spaces. I rolled out my sleeping bag and tucked odds and ends near me on one of the bunks.

"Hey, look, DVDs," Noah said and pointed to a shelf. "Guys, there's movies in here."

"What ones?" Al asked over the rock music. Noah examined the collection.

"*Fight Club, Enemy at the Gates, Freddy Got Fingered*—"

"*Freddy Got Fingered?* Fuck yeah, we're watching that after I beat this. Have you seen it?" Al asked me. I shook my head. "It is hilarious, dude."

"Alright, sounds good to me," I said and took out my journal and pen before I emerged from the v-berth to take a seat at the table. Al nailed his song and high fived Anthony.

"That was awesome!" Anthony crowed. Al held up his big hands.

"I got spiders for hands, man," Al said and flexed his fingers. Noah put in the movie and we all settled in to watch it. I tried to catch up in my journal and watch the movie at the same time, but it was quite a distracting film. In one scene, Tom Greene grabs an erect horse penis and yells, "Look at me Daddy, I'm a farmer!" It's that kind of movie. Al laughed and looked to us to back him up, but Noah and I mostly exchanged awkward glances. When it was all over, Al leapt to his feet and popped out the DVD.

"I remember that being funnier," he said.

The sun was still high in the sky as midnight passed. Scott Brown Jr. didn't join us from the wheelhouse that evening. I imagined him pouring over charts and listening to radio chatter for intel, but he could've been doing Tai Chi in pink moccasins for all I knew. I brushed my teeth and hit the sack. Tomorrow was the first day of fishing.

Tomorrow. What a word; To Morrow. The T starts with a stab and rolls into the Morrow, a snarl tinged with yearning and inevitability. Where is Morrow? Do the people of Morrow dance and love and laugh too loud? Do they murder and lie and fear the dark? To Morrow, indeed.

The sunrise broke over our patch of ocean somewhere near Valdez. My new raingear felt like a bulky rubber potato sack. I looked over to Al to see if I put my stuff on correctly. His bright orange work gloves lay under his jacket sleeves. Mine were over. I copied him and the water guard material of my sleeves hugged my wrists the proper way.

I thought of Al's dad's head injury.

Eighteen years is long enough, right?

Al leaned against the cabin with his hands shoved inside his bib raingear. He nodded to a punk rock song stuck in his head and sucked on a Hot Fireball cinnamon candy. We were both green, but at least Allen Bishop came from this world. Putting me, a kid from the 'burbs who never even heard of seining a month ago, in the same category as this son-of-a-fisherman, fresh-off-another-boat, Alaskan native seemed insulting to Al. If he was green, I was a damned avocado wrapped in spinach leaves dipped in lime juice.

My chest tightened. I was about to go on stage for a performance and I didn't know my lines. What am I doing out here? I wanted to confide in somebody, but none of the somebodies around me would do.

"Yo, what's up with your boots," Al pointed. "Why didn't you get Xtratufs?" I looked down. I hadn't thought of my boots much when I was in G.I. Joes and just grabbed the work boots on sale. They were blue Baffin rain boots.

"Wha? You don't like Bah-fins?" I asked in a vaguely Jersey Shore, 'you wanna go, brah?' accent for some reason. Al smirked.

"I dunno, just never seen 'em before. Everyone I know fishes with Xtratufs," Al said. He pointed to the iconic brown work boots on his feet. What's the worst that could happen? I catch on fire? I didn't know fishermen were so into their brand names.

Noah emerged from the cabin with a tall boy of iced tea in his hand. He wore big-lens sunglasses worthy of LA, and his dark locks hung from his red beanie. His aura was that of a hung-over B-list celebrity and he passed us with a quick nod before he picked over the seine to the skiff. He was a bit jittery, maybe nervous. Possibly just himself.

Whenever I'm nervous, I get sleepy. It is as if my body says, nope, I'm checking out. Let me know how it goes, and powers down. So, thankfully, I don't think I looked too nervous, just reasonably tired early in the morning. Al was at home, one cool cat. Who was I to disrupt the vibe?

The *Solstice* idled patiently.

I stretched.

Yaaawwwn…

Scott Brown Jr. swung open the door onto the bridge and climbed down the ladder to join us. He wore a black sweater under his orange Grundens raingear and a faded green baseball cap on his shaved head. We were in fjord country and the verdant green sides of the mountains rose straight out of the Sound around us, great fingers scooping us up in a giant's palm. The other seiners idled as we did, ready for six o' clock and the opener. Scott studied the scenery for a few seconds with an outward calm and inward intensity. He glanced at his watch before he muttered something unintelligible in my general direction. I could barely make out his eyes from behind his sunglasses.

"Time to fish," Scott finally declared and turned back to the wheelhouse. So began my often-painful metamorphosis from landlubber to deckhand, from a useless individual with daydreams and free will to an invaluable tool with a job to do. From greenhorn to old hand. I had me some learn' to do.

It is best to think of commercial salmon seining as a team sport, not unlike American football. Football has positions like the quarterback, the receiver, and the linemen who each play a role in a successful down. A fully crewed salmon seiner has the skipper, the skiffman, and the deckhands to pull off a successful set. The game has a football with which to score points. The livelihood has a living ball of salmon with which to make money. Football teams play each other and salmon seining vessels are in competition for limited resources.

Football players make millions and risk concussions.

Fishermen make thousands, sometimes, and risk their lives.

Football players gain national fame and roll in babes.

Fishermen... never mind.

The point is that everybody is a piece of the machine with specific roles to master. Our skipper, Scott Brown Jr., called the play for us deckhands (Al and I) and the skiffman (Noah) to execute while he drove the seiner and operated the hydraulic machinery. Not all skippers manned the hydraulics, but Scott Brown Jr. did. He believed that the hydraulics were too dangerous for greenhorns.

While the ocean is a large place, there are highly desirable areas near spawning streams for salmon seining. These streams are natural bottlenecks for the desperately horny salmon migrating up the stream of their conception to spawn and therefore magnets for us insatiable humans. To avoid all-out war over those bottlenecks, seiner captains strictly followed an unwritten code of conduct to maximize profit for all. The penalty of breaking the code was the ultimate punishment at sea; the worsening of one's reputation. Reputation was everything to a skipper, for few things were worse than being dubbed an asshole by the fleet at large. If a skipper cut somebody off in the lineup, the offense could cause multigenerational resentment and accusations of asshole to fly. A skipper who liked you may lend you a spare something if you really needed it. A skipper who thought you were an asshole might keep fishing. For every opportunity to gain face, there were three to lose it.

I never heard anybody label Scott Brown Jr. an asshole.

The orderly lines of seiners formed at the desirable spots on a first come, first-served basis, free of any official regulation but subject to the sacred unwritten code. Everybody got a turn in the cycle to set their net in the best spot and it was each vessel's duty to work the area efficiently and move out of the way to keep the line moving. A skipper had rights to a second set near the good spot if the first one went smoothly. If it took too long to retrieve the gear due to Murphy's Law—all that can go wrong will go wrong—or the catch was so full of salmon the vessel couldn't pull it aboard in a timely manner, it was an honorable skipper's job to opt out of his or her second set.

The line had to keep moving and good feelings depended on everybody playing nice and playing fast. As a deckhand, the length of the lineup translated to various amounts of waiting. If the line was long, I waited more than an hour between sets. These breaks were excellent opportunities to take off my slimy gloves and lounge on the seine. Or chill in the cabin with an iced tea tallboy and a bag of chips to shoot the breeze with Noah, who was with the main group when the skiff didn't demand his attention. When it was our turn in the lineup, Scott stomped on the cabin ceiling from above in the wheelhouse.

"Get ready!" He'd roar. It was the only part of the process where Scott regularly raised his voice at us. We were lucky he wasn't a screamer. Things would've been very different aboard the *Sharon* under Captain Rick, who I wasn't surprised to hear was regularly labeled an asshole. Scott Brown Sr. was a screamer. I knew that the *Mantis* was near when I heard him growlcuss over the water.

After Scott Brown Jr.'s command, Al and I donned our slimy orange work gloves while Noah scurried into the skiff. The skiff was a jet-powered aluminum tub the *Solstice* towed. When Scott deemed the moment ripe, we set the skiff loose by flipping a pin on the bear-trap-like skiff release to disconnect the towline. The two ends of the seine net were attached to the two boats and, when the skiff's towline was disconnected, the two vessels motored apart to stretch the seine around a school of salmon.

The seine, which up to this point was an unholy heap of gear on the deck, started to unravel off the stern into the sea. Al and I hung out with our hands in our pockets forward of the action. We kept an eye out for any snags and made sure everything set smoothly.

I learned that getting tangled in an outgoing seine was one of the most common ways for deckhands to die. A drag across the deck with one's leg caught in the webbing was enough to break bone and the entrapment underwater in the North Pacific was usually impossible to undo with the hydraulics. Once trapped underwater, the deckhand's only hope was the reaction of witnesses. If they were not quick with their skiffs and knives, he died of his wounds and asphyxiation. If rescued, he'd likely become hypothermic. The seine hissed like a cobra when it travelled over the deck and I gave it the same space and respect. Scott said he'd tear us a new asshole if we went too close.

Once set, the seine was brilliant in its simplicity. Three lines manipulated the thick black webbing of the net. The cork line strung floats to keep the top side of the seine afloat, while a thick heavy lead line sunk the bottom side. These two opposing lines stretched the webbing to its maximum and corralled salmon in the water column. Meanwhile, the purse line ran through a series of metal rings that hung from the submerged lead-line edge of the seine. The important purse line was tightened by hydraulic deck winch at the proper moment to close the bottom of the seine like, well, a purse.

Perhaps if salmon possessed more conniving, man-like minds, they would simply leap over the cork line and out of the seine. Luckily for man, we are the masters of murderous genius. Salmon have only one thought, to spawn, and they charge bravely across hostile territory to often-horrific deaths for the cause. See my previous thoughts on the stupid courage a one percent chance can give a romantic.

The seiner and the skiff held positions for a good twenty minutes for the seine to soak. Noah usually positioned the skiff near shore, the nearer the better for land was an absolute barrier against which to entrap a school of fish. After Scott set the seine as long as he could without upsetting the lineup, Noah was ordered to return in order to close the circle of the net with the seiner.

Noah delivered his end of the net to the deck in exchange for a towline from me. Scott shut off the engine so our propeller wouldn't tear up the net as we made the preparations to wrestle it on deck. With the *Solstice* dead in the water, it was up to Noah to tow us clear of shore and dangerous obstacles. The pressure on him at this point was minimal as the rest of us sweated to secure the bacon.

Now the fate of the salmon school was largely sealed. The fish could not swim laterally due to the webbing stretched by the cork and lead lines, and could not dive deeper due to the tightened purse line. The only opening in the seine existed directly under the boat and it was the deckhand's job to attack the water with 12-foot-long aluminum plungers to dissuade the entrapped salmon. These plungers made a smacking *pop* when they hit the water. The idea was the plunger noises helped deter the salmon from the critical opening.

Scott demonstrated proper plunging technique during our first set. He thrust the alien probe into the water. *Pop!* The shaft slid through his hands until the plunger was almost lost. He gripped the end of the shaft tightly and drew the plunger back up for another thrust.

"See? Not hard," Scott said and handed me the plunger. I sent about plunging with Al, who was already practiced. I hit the water.

Pop! The shaft slid through my hands and I drew the plunger for another strike.

Pop! "Yeah, this isn't hard at all," I declared.

Pop! The metal shaft slid through my hands.

"Yeah, I can do this… oh no!" The entire shaft slid through my grasp and the plunger fell into the sea. We scrambled to retrieve it, but it was gone. Plunger down. I promised I'd find another. Scott said he was ready to charge me eighty bucks if I didn't by the end of the season.

The seine was fed into the power block, a large mechanical pulley suspended over the deck by the seiner's signature arm boom. This massive workhorse brought in the seine and it was the deckhand's primary duty to guide the two edges of the net (the cork line and the side with the lead and purse lines) to the deck in a useable, orderly manner. Everything thus far was preparation for this moment. It was up to the brawn and quick hands of Al and me to actually get salmon into the boat. Touchdown.

Scott typically loomed over the hydraulics panel, his hands itching for the switches. Al and I positioned aft of him and stood side-by-side under the power block. Al stood to the starboard flank where the cork line came down. I manned to port where the lead and purse lines attacked. Scott would give the scene a quick but thorough scan.

We were attached to a giant pile of living money if we didn't screw this up.

"Ready?" Scott would ask. Al and I nodded and the power block came to life above us from where it hung on the arm boom. The loud, terrifying machinery cranked up the net from the sea and spat it down onto us. Al and

I grabbed our lines as soon as they were within reach and drew curving S patterns with them on the deck as we worked toward the stern. Flaking they called it. With every length of seine secured on deck, the salmon grew more constricted in the purse. Victory neared. If we didn't do a good job, the lead and cork lines could get tangled in the next set. Not good. Salmon would swim right through the mess we made. Money out of our pockets.

Sometimes a doomed salmon tangled its gills in the webbing and passed through the power block. Ideally, I could pick out the giller before it was buried in the gear at my feet. But sometimes that just wasn't possible, and the mangled silver beastie was buried alive under thousands of pounds of gear where it turned rancid if left alone. Maybe it would rot off the seine eventually. The fate of a deckhand falling behind his line was not so different.

Al and I had many enemies, one of which was tunnel vision. I was tempted to devote all my attention to the river of webbing and line passing through my hands, but I had to keep my head on a swivel. Not only could misplaced gear tangle the next set but stacking the gear onto my feet could put me in an even more dangerous situation. When working fast it only took a few seconds of standing in the wrong place to be wrapped in webbing above one's knees, a perilous position that required a holler for help. The power block had to be stopped while the deckhand got his act together. The flow was interrupted. The money stopped.

To be the reason the power block wasn't moving fast was loathsome.

To be the slow one was to be the weakest link.

This was no place for weakness.

I also had to be aware of what came out of the power block above. Bundles of line, commonly known as clusterfucks, passed through the block and fell en masse. If a deckhand wasn't careful when working directly under the block, hundreds of pounds of gear laced with metal purse line rings could fall on him like a coiled anaconda. Goodnight.

Jellyfish were another scourge. The gelatinous stinging bastards clung to the webbing like giant snot balls. A jellyfish sting felt like that annoying kid in your middle school class who snapped you in the arm with a rubber band. But the snapping lasted for hours. If a piece of jellyfish got in an eye, one could be half-blind for the day. I often glanced at our seine in the water for a glimpse of the haul and my eyes widened with horror when I beheld approaching webbing coated with translucent orange goo. The grinding power block pulverized the jellies into stinging rain.

"Jellyfish!" Al often raised the call. I'd give my rubber hood a good tug over my head and look down at my feet. According to Herodotus, Dienekes, the bravest of the 300 Spartans at Thermopylae, jested that when the Persian arrows blotted out the sun, the Greeks should rejoice for they would fight in the shade. I don't think the jellyfish rain ever blotted out the sun, but I hid under my rubber hood like a hoplite under his bronze shield at the Hot Gates quite often. I certainly never rejoiced. A poorly timed upward peek risked a painful protoplasmic fist to the face. This happened to me on the first day. I turned to Scott after the set was done. My right cheek was red and puffy, my vision blurred with tears.

"Scott… what do I do?" I asked. A second's pause.

"Don't look up," Scott replied. I never brought up jellyfish stings again on-deck and now scowl at them when I visit aquariums. Seawater also ended up in my eyes. Come to think of it, I remember many of the sets as a series of painful blurs and grinding mechanical noises. My eyes were often red afterward like somebody who didn't wear goggles in an overly chlorinated pool.

To improve time was the endless goal and to beat the power block's maximum capabilities was the dream. In the beginning I often thought about how satisfying it would be to smirk at Scott as I easily bested the power block at its fastest. Perhaps there is something innately American about building machines and trying to best our creations with bare hands and strong backs like John Henry. So it was that Al and I gritted teeth against falling clusterfucks, jellyfish, webbing at our feet, and our own muscles with Yankee ambitions in our perpetual race against the power block and seine. Scott Brown Jr. always gave us more speed if things were going smoothly and we looked too comfortable.

Next the time came for the final phase of the struggle. The captured school of salmon was confined to the last corner of the purse called the bunt. Al and I caught our breaths and opened the hatch covers to the hold, a giant refrigerator held in the gut of the seiner. Seiners are essentially floating refrigerators and the hold was pumped with chilled seawater to preserve the fish until delivery to a larger floating refrigerator/processing boat known as a tender. The freezing seawater was usually what killed the salmon, a more humane death than most.

At this point Al and I either whooped with victory at a good haul or grimaced at our tiny catch. The price for pink salmon at the beginning of the 2008 season was twenty-five cents per pound. Ten percent of each haul was mine. I kept dutiful notes complete with calculations of our running tonnage.

The typical catch was a manageable few thousand pounds and the power block could lift the salmon directly into the hold. Scott was a master at the hydraulics. He teased the writhing loads expertly into the frigid coffin. Al and I guided the suspended ball of struggling muscle and slime as best we could. The ball opened and a stream of silver scales and fins and yellow eyes and gaping toothed mouths flowed into the hold. Al and I pitched the dozens, sometimes hundreds, of salmon that spilled across the deck into the hold to join the others. Cha-ching.

The set was a wrap at this point. Al and I stowed the rest of the gear. Scott went back to the wheelhouse and 'round went the props. Noah returned with the skiff and we secured it to the bear-trap release. Al or I hosed off the deck.

A special kind of marine mucus collected on deck, a mixture of seawater, crushed jellyfish, silver scales, and dashes of fish blood. There probably should be a name for this oceanic smegma, but I never heard it. Maybe I should've bottled it up and sold it as a cosmetic gel to yuppies.

The ritual repeated. We waited in line for the next set. We took off the slimy work gloves. We cracked open iced teas and wolfed down Chex Mix. Scott announced the next set. I'd feel like throwing up. The ritual repeated.

We bullied our way through a couple of sets that first day. Of course, I lost my plunger. Noah got messed up in the seine once. Al and I were still no match for even a modest power block pace. The wind picked up and we were worried about tearing the gear in the water, so Scott called the day off early. We motored to Valdez to check out the seine and assess the damage we greenhorns had caused. Somehow it didn't amount to anything out of the ordinary. Scott turned us loose late in the afternoon.

"Good job, guys. If we can get the speed up, which we will with practice, we're going to have a great season," he said with calm, contagious confidence. I believed him and quietly vowed to replace the plunger I lost.

Valdez Rhythm and the Fourth of July

"Where you going?" I asked Al. He glanced back at me with a purple beanie on his head and skateboard under his arm. We just back hauled the seine, which meant running the gear through the power block in reverse. Collectively we picked a few mangled gillers, but there was no real damage. We greenhorns didn't cause too much harm.

"Skate park, man, and then I'll probably crash my uncle's place. Catchya later," Al said. He hopped on his skateboard. I wouldn't see him until it was time to go tomorrow, skinny jeans and all. I shrugged and turned to Noah who was also leaving the boat.

"What about you?" I asked.

"I gotta see what Johnny is up to on the *Sil-Ver-Fish*," Noah said.

"The *Sil-Ver-Fish*? You know, they almost hired me," I said.

"Yeah, I heard. Some of my friends are on board. Those dummies are hilarious," Noah chuckled as he walked away. "Word is they're broken down already and might be out for the season."

"Really? Already?" I heaved a big sigh. If Scott Brown Jr. hadn't called me when he did, my season would be over after one day. I bid Noah farewell. Anthony stood patiently at my side.

"What about you, big man?" I asked. "Doing something?"

"Not really," Anthony shrugged.

"Well…" I gestured to my bag of laundry. "I'm going to do laundry after I take a shower. Do you know where that is? Want to take a walk?"

"Hecka yeah, nigga," Anthony said.

"Don't say that word, Anthony," I muttered ineffectually and we were off on the town. Valdez was bigger than Cordova, but not by much. In fact, the differences between the two towns arose primarily because Valdez was attached to the US Interstate Highway System and boasted a heavily guarded oil-processing district. I presume that this led to more accessibility, jobs, schools, skate parks, people, crime, Subways, Starbucks, internet, etc. Isolated Cordova chugged along almost exclusively by its fishing economy. As a consequence, Cordova seemed to be shrinking and Valdez to be growing. Capitalists rejoice.

I stopped by the harbormaster who sold four-dollar tokens for the showers.

"Outrageous," I muttered as I entered the showers. Anthony skipped around the marina. There were only a few stalls, but luckily one was open. A bearded tattooed man, a sort of pirate Jesus, was readying to enter the last shower. Our eyes met and I was about to turn around.

"Hey brother, you want to use this?" He asked.

I waved him off.

"Nah, man, you got here first," I said.

"No, brother. I insist," said Pirate Jesus. He turned away from the showers and grabbed his towel. "You're a deckhand, right? I'm a deckhand on the *Tacoma*."

"Yeah, I'm on the *Solstice*. You don't have to do this, man, you were first." He rested his hand on my shoulder. I calmed. Pirate Jesus' brown eyes were shiny and benevolent, but urgent, like he needed me to understand something important. Was that the shimmer of a halo above his head?

"The universe won't be a better place unless we all do our part, brother," Pirate Jesus said. My voice almost escaped me.

"I suppose so," I trailed off. Pirate Jesus nodded and left me to think in the shower.

Anthony and I tackled the town properly after my rinse. He guided me to the Laundromat a few blocks from the marina. We swung by the change machines for quarters and the vending machines of soapboxes. I paid. My clothes got blasted. I turned to Anthony who was sticking his skinny arms up a soap-dispensing machine.

"Anthony, what are you doing?" I asked.

Anthony, grinning, held up a box of detergent.

"Look. You can get them for free!" He tucked the prize under his arm and started to fish for more. Anthony was giddy with discovery, adorable in a mischievous goblin sort of way. The bell on the door rang. Pirate Jesus entered.

"Hello, brother," freshly showered Pirate Jesus greeted with a benevolent bearded smile and a load of dirty laundry.

"Look," Anthony said and held up a second soapbox. "Free!" Pirate Jesus shook his head.

"That ain't honest, little man. And you better watch out for that bad karma. It will catch up to you, sooner or later," he said. Anthony glowered and we left. I felt like I let the universe down. We heathens didn't walk far before Anthony leapt up and pointed to a vacant lot on the other side of the street. A black and white rabbit nibbled at grasses poking between rusty leavings.

"It's a bunny! A bunny, a bunny," Anthony chanted. We tiptoed across the road. "I want it," he hissed.

"Well, we're going to need to get some carrots or something for bait and be really nice to her," I said. "Then maybe she'll like us and become a good pet."

"Yeah, or…" Anthony trailed off. He dropped onto his hands and knees and slunk toward the rabbit. He didn't get far before she bolted. "Damn it, nigga!"

"Anthony!" I scolded. "Don't say that!"

Anthony needed to meet his dad on the *Mantis* for a Brown family meal, so we parted ways. I found Noah and the crew of the *Sil-Ver-Fish* aboard the *Solstice*.

"Hey, Norris," Noah greeted me. A husky, scruffy kid with a baseball cap over wild orange hair and a big smile was at Noah's side.

"Norris! It's Johnny, man. I almost hired you," Johnny said.

"Hey," I laughed and we shook hands. "Yeah, sorry about that. Scott snapped me up."

"No problem, man. This is a good boat," Johnny nodded.

"Unlike yours?" Noah offered. The crowd sniggered. Johnny put his hands up in defensive surrender.

"Hey, where's your boat, bro? Where's. *Your*. Boat? Hmmm?" Johnny retorted. I learned later that Johnny was seventeen, an ambitious and brave age to start skippering. The saying about books and their covers comes to mind. I admit, I actually do judge books by their covers. The sleekest covers almost always cover the cheapest stories.

"We're going on a hike. The trail is behind the school. Do you want to come?" Noah asked.

"Sure," I said. We walked across town to behind the school where a trail wound its way up the green muddy flanks of a mountain. We hiked up it for a while, everybody exhausted and unprepared, before giving up. They split up to get ready for a second attempt, but I was too hungry and went to the *Solstice* to chow down.

I made a mental note to give the trail an honest try the next chance I got as I scrounged about the boat for a meal and watched the foot traffic of Valdez pass. An out-of-place pair of young women walked by the docks. Long legs and booty shorts. Low cut shirts and big sunglasses. They walked like celebrities, aloof to the world that was a backdrop to their lives. An old man on a bicycle pedaled full speed behind them and leaned in close enough to lick one of their ears.

"Boo!" He yelled at the top of his lungs. They screamed and leapt into each other's arms. Their platinum blonde ironed hair frizzed. The soft parts of their bodies jiggled. They belly laughed in the aftermath of sheer terror. It was memorable, maybe even important, but I'm not sure why. Pirate Jesus, wherever he ended up, may have the answer.

July 4, 0430 hours. The cell phone alarm buzzed on the tiny shelf by my head, the screen alight. My eyes struggled open to a dark v-berth and I writhed on top of my sleeping bag in pure agony. I told the guys I made a mean breakfast. It was time to show them.

Yeesh.

I seized the trembling phone and rolled out of bed, my face contorted into a miserable scowl. Mornings. Suck. Noah and Al were lumps of sweet bliss in their sleeping bags. I stumbled bleary eyed to the galley.

I fumbled with butter from the fridge and slices of bread.

I turned on the propane stovetop and selected a drinking glass of the proper size for my purpose.

I pressed it into the nearest bread slice and twisted a hole in the center before plucking the bread circle out of the cup's lip.

I put the bread, both circle and hole, onto a frying pan that sat on a low, blue flame.

I cracked an egg into the hole of the bread slice and reached for a spatula.

Happy Birthday, 'Murica, I saluted inwardly to the sizzle-hiss of breakfast.

"That's what you were boasting about, huh? Egg in a basket?" Noah joined me, somehow chipper. I placed an open jar of strawberry jam on the table and rubbed my eyes.

"Yup, except I always knew them as bull's eyes," I said, a zombie holding a spatula. Dawn crept into the cabin through the portholes as I dished up a stack. The first few bull's eyes were burnt, so I turned the heat down a little.

Al joined us, his fists rubbing his eyes. Anthony teetered down the ladder from the wheelhouse. The little guy was pretty cute in the morning when he was too sleepy to bounce off the walls or set something on fire. He looked at the plate of bull's eyes Noah and I dug into.

"Toad in a hole," Anthony said as he forked one on his plate.

"Norris calls them bull's eyes," Noah said. "What do you call them, Al? My family calls them egg in a basket."

"I don't know man... fuck'n..." Al grumbled and shoveled two onto his plate. "Glory holes." We sniggered, even Anthony, although I doubt he knew what a glory hole was. I turned to the ladder to see Scott descending. He sat next to Anthony at the table.

"We've got first set in the lineup, just so you know," Scott said and put three bull's eyes on a plate. "Be ready at six." We nodded. There was one bull's eye left. I thought about making more, but Noah was already doing the dishes. I figured I might as well hang out on the deck. I put on my hoodie and eased into my raingear. My jacket and gloves could wait until we were ready to set. I went onto the deck alone after slipping on my blue boots, the lone pair of bargain Baffins in a Xtratuf world.

Scott kept the *Solstice* at an easy idle a few football fields away from the entrance to Shoup Bay. I could see the *Mantis* and maybe six other boats in the lineup behind us. I had no doubt that a familiar scene played on each of the boats, with sleepy crew stumbling into positions and anxious skippers biting their lips in their wheelhouses.

The small fleet of neighboring vessels were about all I could see. The morning fog was so thick that the line between sea and sky was wiped out. I lounged on the seine and watched the other boats suspended in a grey cloud too frigid and salty to be the heaven the Bible talked about. Still, I couldn't shake the feeling we were plucked from the ocean and made airborne somehow. I sat in a cold hypnotic peace. The work to come would warm me up and the sun would burn the fog away eventually. We'd be back on Earth.

"Get ready!" Scott's cry to arms sent Noah and Al onto the deck. Noah scampered over the seine to the skiff and Al hung out at the deck winch, hands in his pockets and Fireball candy in his mouth. We were all too sleepy to say anything, but we were ready. Scott motored the *Solstice* in the direction of land and left the other boats to hover in the cloud behind us. I donned my work jacket and gloves. Al and I exchanged nods as the *Solstice* turned her stern to shore. I put my hand on the pin for the bear trap release.

Show time, 'Murica.

"Go!" Scott yelled over the engine. I threw the pin. The bear trap released with a satisfying clang. I stowed the now useless thing clear of the workspace while Noah motored off with his end of the seine.

Perfect takeoff. Noah drove the skiff to the beach and the seine arched beautifully between us. Al blasted the deck with the hose. Foul smelling ocean smegma from previous sets washed into the sea. I coiled a towline. Noah would come alongside after giving us his end of the seine and I'd throw this towline into the skiff. He'd grab a hold of the yellow float clip on the end, attach it to the proper part of the skiff, and tow us clear of danger while we turned off the prop and wrestled the net onto the boat.

If I missed my throw, we would float helplessly until I recovered the line and got it into Noah's hands. Noah sometimes motored right up alongside and I could hand him the line, but he was usually in a hurry and motored past for the transfer ten feet or more from me. It was only a few seconds of the set, but all eyes were on me for the throw. The last thing I was going to worry about was a tangle in the towline, so I learned to flake out the line into coils before sets. This time I somehow turned a small knot into a pile of mating garter snakes, a real clusterfuck in the works. Al looked on.

"You got that, man? Here, I think you should—" he began.

"I got it, thanks man," I said, ears red. I kept fumbling around like the landlubber I was. Al shrugged and dropped it. I straightened things out after ten or so minutes of silent rage. Al would've cleared it in no time. I was still pretty stressed from the mess when Noah came to close the seine. Scott joined us on deck.

"We're going to go quick on this one and take our second set. I saw the school up there and we just nicked it with this one." I exchanged a look with Al.

"Sounds good," I said. Nothing I could've said would've mattered. Noah handed off his side of the seine and motored around to receive the towline. I chucked the yellow float with an overhand throw. It sailed a good fifteen feet.

Clunk! Right into the boat.

Bull's Eye. Toad in the hole. Egg in the muthfuckin' basket. Noah scrambled to attach the clip. Al and I got into our positions under the power block. Scott fed line to the deck winch and hovered his hand over the hydraulic switches.

"Ready?" Scott asked. We nodded and the power block roared to life above us. Al and I grabbed our lines and began the real work. My lead line was sometimes twisted up in the webbing and I gave it a flick like how Scott taught me to free it. The pile of gear at our feet grew.

"Going faster," Scott said. The power block groaned as it spun. I moved my hands with an animal's desperation. To fall behind meant death. Talons upon the mouse. Al's cork piles were textbook beautiful. The lead line never looked good, but at least I didn't feel like I made a mess of the seine.

"Full speed?" Scott suggested. "Let's see if you can keep up with the machine."

"Let's see if the machine can keep up with us!" I retorted through pants. Scott snorted.

"This machine will kick your ass, boy," he said and cranked up the speed to its max.

"Fuck yeah," Al grinned for the first few seconds before his smile vanished. Then I could only look at my hands.

Grab, grab, grab, twist, grab, grab, grab, twist, twist.

I moved as fast as I could, but I dropped the line after a few minutes and it swung toward Al. Scott slowed down while I recovered. We met eyes and I nodded to show that I had the situation under control. He sped up again but spared us maximum speed. Al's piles looked a bit sloppy, but at least he had kept up. I gritted my teeth for the rest of the set, still the slowest on deck but learning.

Noah returned from towing us and lounged in the skiff for the next set. Scott, quiet but moving fast, motored to where we had rights to our second set. The *Mantis* was closing up their first set on the beach behind us. Speed was going to be important for this one if we were going to keep the line moving. I poised over the bear trap.

"Go!" Scott called. Noah motored away. Al blasted the deck with the hose. I coiled the towline for my throw. Noah came close and I threw the towline, clunk, right into the skiff.

Bull's eye. Toad in the hole. Egg in the muthafuckin' basket. I once again struggled with the slithering serpent of lead line under the power block grind. A jellyfish bounced off my shoulder and a little piece of it stung my lower lip. I deadened my mind for another long, chaotic wrestling match with the seine, but Scott started to slow. I looked up. I was doing fine for once. Al's corks were gorgeous, a true work of art. What's the hold up?

"Fuck yeah!" Al crowed. I craned my neck to look off his side of the boat where the seine soaked in the water. My mouth dropped. We were just a few minutes into this set and already fish bulged at the sides of the great tea bag. Scott pulled in the rest of the net nice and slow. The whole boat heaved to the side under the weight with a groan and a splash. We crowded against the rail to look at our haul.

"We're going to need a bigger boat," I muttered the *Jaws* reference under my breath.

"I'm calling in the tender. We're going to offload right out of the net," Scott said and was off to the radio in the wheelhouse. A tender loomed out of the dispersing fog and came alongside after a few minutes. The trapped salmon were sandwiched between us. The tender's vacuum tube lowered into the net.

"Hey!" Scott pointed to where the cork line was doubling up under the crush of the two-vessel sandwich. Whole lengths of sunk cork line offered the pressed salmon an escape route. Scott gathered the deckhands.

"We have to keep the slack out of this thing or we're going to lose most of it. Grab a handful! Pull!" Scott ordered. I sank my digits into a piece of webbing, planted my feet on the gunnel, and dead lifted a length of net onto the deck. Then I grabbed another and did the same. And another. I could feel every fish in the web like I was a spider who caught a thousand flies. Scott looked on without feedback and kept the vacuum tube in place, no doubt happy about the salmon bodies thumping through it. I was content in my productive misery as long as he was satisfied. When I caught up with the slack, I gritted my teeth and held the tension. My arms were rubber by the end of it, but there had been 23,000 pounds of salmon in that one set alone. Al high-fived me.

"Some balls, man!" Al said and smiled ear to ear.

"Balls! Yes!" I exclaimed. "'Murica!" The day was a long one, plagued by monkey-wrench tasks such as this, but the haul was good. An opener usually ended promptly at 1800 hours. That's it, that's the law. Pull in the gear and you were done for the day, right? Not for a deckhand. If the hold was full at the end of the day, like ours on that Fourth of July, it was time to deliver the fish to the tender.

The final critical step where fish became money was exceptionally important, so every skipper in the fleet rushed to the nearest tender hired by the company with which he or she had a contract. This lineup was usually very long, for the whole fleet descended upon the handful of tenders often an hour or so before the official closing. If we fished right up to 1800 hours, we forgot about going to bed early. Best make some dinner and get comfortable in line. This was usually when Al proved himself to be the best at Guitar Hero, his long spidery fingers a distinct advantage. I was awful. Even Anthony was better than me.

Delivering the fish wasn't ever very fun, but it was a satisfying end to a day of work that Fourth of July. The *Solstice* came along a hulking 100-plus foot tender, probably a repurposed crabber up from Dutch Harbor making some cash between crab seasons. We deckhands removed the hatch covers from the hold and guided a monstrous vacuum tube inside. The gigantic flaccid proboscis was big enough to suck up Anthony.

We deckhands watched the foam broth of seawater and dying salmon vanish up the tube until we could go into the hold and not flood our boots. The vacuum needed help to get all the fish out, and Al, Noah, and I jumped in with short shovels to be that help. We jumped in too soon on the fourth and icy water flowed over my boots and numbed my feet. Near-freezing brine sprayed from the jets above and the shriek of the jets and the vacuum echoed in the frigid chamber to drown out everything else. A gaping mouth full of jagged teeth or a yellow eye sometimes emerged from the foam, a salmon on the edge of death. I would poke him or her into the tube and then he or she was away, bound for the cannery and some distant human's gut. If the fish weighed a typical three pounds, I made about seven cents. On that Fourth of July, there were so many salmon in the hold that I stood in a river of them. Beautiful silver dragons. My shovel was a blur as every one of the fish ended up the tube.

We caught 57,000 pounds of salmon that day, by far our best day of the season to that point. At twenty-five cents a pound, each crewmember made about $1,400. We started delivering at around 0100 hours on July 5 after a long wait in line. It took about forty minutes to deliver our catch and I reckon we hit the sack at around 0200 hours. There was an opener coming up the next day, so we would have to be up at 0500 hours to gear up and be on deck for work at 0600. Independence Day fireworks from Valdez popped a muffled lullaby, but we couldn't see them. I noticed Scott chugging from a box of cheap red wine but didn't think too much of it at the time. I never felt so patriotic in my life, the usual backyard barbeque with the folks and sparklers suddenly a staged performance compared to this raw slam poetry injection of the U.S. of A.

I woke up a few hours later in a cold sweat on a restless *Solstice*. Fifty-knot winds made her shudder on her anchor in the dark. I dreamt of fishing. I was in the hold up to my chest in freezing water and coercing salmon into the vacuum tube with my shovel. The salmon had human faces and their jaws moved up and down noiselessly, dying as they swam in lethargic resistance. I forced an endless silver flood of the salmon people, men and women, into the void of the vacuum and watched their gasping faces shake in horrified surprise. They were spat into a radiant cosmos of galaxies above me.

Fisherman's Life for Me

A closure was announced and we back hauled the seine outside of Shoup Bay to check for tears and gillers. Scott was the only one with proper net mending skills, so he, with threader in hand, danced across the slowly moving webbing to tend to small holes. He told us of when he first learned how to net mend. Scott was sixteen and the seine of the boat he worked on had been ripped, almost to shreds. The skipper's wife handed Scott a threader and worked with him all day on the repair. Scott must've been in a good mood, because he also told us another story about how they somehow gilled nineteen salmon sharks in one set.

"We cut off the fuckers' fins and put them back," Scott said flatly. "They didn't eat our salmon anymore." Al smirked. My jaw almost dropped. Was the 57,000 pounds of yesterday not enough? Like the wolf and the rancher, there was no love spared between the fisherman and the shark. I dearly hoped we wouldn't catch any sharks, for I knew I'd make a scene by refusing to partake in the massacre.

We motored to Valdez after the back haul was complete. Al disappeared to the skate park. Scott and Anthony joined the Brown family somewhere. Noah went off with his *Sil-Ver-Fish* buddies. I had the ultimate bachelor dinner for one: homemade deer hot dogs, pop tarts, and an iced tea tallboy.

I looked through our DVD collection and was surprised to find a few pornos complete with cover sleeves of platinum blondes licking their balloon-shaped tits and touching themselves over G-string thongs. More femme-bot than woman, I suppose, but what was I going to do, organize a street protest about body positivity? I was tempted to pop one in and jerk it, being human and all, but the potential shame of a surprise return of somebody was too much of a risk. I sighed and spent my alone time reading and pining after high school crushes.

Something of a routine began to develop. Shoup Bay emerged as our money maker. We usually got a day or two or three of openers before the Alaska Fish and Wildlife folks said the fish counts were too low. A one- or two-day closer would be announced and we'd run back to Valdez to indulge in luxuries like laundry and four-dollar showers. We'd wait in Valdez for the next noontime announcement to declare an opener and then race the other boats to be first in the lineup at Shoup. Scott was all about being first in line at Shoup. The 23,000-pound first set on the Fourth of July spoke for itself. I reckon the *Solstice* must've been a pretty fast boat, for we left most of the other seiners in our wake during opener races.

One day I was working at the stern, probably checking out the seine for some reason as it soaked, and a sea lion rose from the green depths next to me. A male Stellar, bigger than an African lion by at least 200 pounds. Maybe 500. He likely had bigger teeth than a lion too. We locked eyes before he puffed a foul-smelling mist in my direction and took a breath. Whiskers, a bloodshot eye roll, a flap of flippers, and the visitor was gone. I kept up my work. I heard some skippers, Scott Brown Jr. included, complain about the sea lions eating fish out of their nets. If it weren't for the Marine Mammal Protection Act, I reckon the sea lions would all be long dead, shot between the eyes and left to float for the sake of a few pounds of salmon.

Anthony's black-market soap store was in fine shape under my bunk. Inventory was maxed out after every trip to Valdez, but business was poor for a few reasons. Firstly, his market was tiny, just us crew of the *Solstice*. Second, he refused to lower his prices below what land offered. I was his only loyal customer. When we visited Valdez, I'd buy my soaps from Anthony, go to the Laundromat, and put a dollar into the vending machine without making a selection. It was in this way that I supported Anthony's entrepreneurial spirit and alleviated my conscience.

In Pirate Jesus' name we pray.

Not all the days were compliant with our goals. The 57,000 pounds of the Fourth of July had set an unreasonable expectation. Most days fell short. July 6 yielded a mere 15,200 pounds, a more typical haul. The price of pink salmon, also known as humpies, went up to twenty-seven cents per pound, which was welcome news. Still, I could sense Scott's frustration. He was more prone to let conversations die mid-sentence and it was increasingly common for an empty box of wine to fall from the wheelhouse into the sea. Yet he remained calm and patient, even though Al, Noah, and I still climbed the learning curve. I was usually the slower one on deck, but I didn't want to stay that way and gave it my all.

Fuck ups happened. Once a cork line got trapped in the webbing and sank. Was one of us deckhands at fault for not flaking the seine properly, or was this just Murphy's Law in action? Scott watched the salmon swim out of the net while my stomach churned.

"Cocksucker," he muttered and pushed the machine to go faster to retrieve the gear so we would stop wasting time on a doomed set. Al and I did our best. By the time the net came up, there wasn't a single fish in the net.

"Not your fault," Scott assured us.

I desperately hoped he meant it.

71

One evening before an opener, Scott Brown Jr. made tortellini with deer sausage while we drifted on the hook, anchor in sailor speak. The steaming pot of ambrosia sat on the table as Scott ladled up our bowls. Al and Anthony bickered over the plastic guitar.

"I've never had deer before I came up here," I said after my first bite. "It's awesome."

"Never?" Scott gasped. "You're from Oregon, there's deer all over there. Just walk outside and shoot one."

"I've never gone hunting before." I looked into my bowl as I shoveled the delicious slop. "I've never shot a gun before either."

"Never?" Scott was dumbstruck. He suggested that I immediately get a .22 rifle like the one Anthony had above his bunk in the wheelhouse. I said I'd think about it.

Talk turned to money, the topic always on Scott's mind. He had been out of sorts the last few days because Scott Brown Sr. had canceled his contract with one of the seafood companies on account of their not providing him tender support in the middle of an opener. Senior almost lost thousands of pounds-worth of fish that needed delivering and tore up his contract in a rage. The company wasn't pleased and tried to bring him back into the fold. No dice, Senior wasn't the type to budge. He had expected Junior to join in his strike, but that didn't happen. Father-son tensions were high.

Scott made sense in a sort of epiphany as I polished off bowl number three of deer tortellini. He was ruined if salmon weren't caught and money wasn't made, wiped out in a way that was completely alien to the salaried landlubber adults in whose shadows I had grown. He had to make $100,000 a season just to break even. Until that $100,000 was made, he was drowning in red ink. If a season or two were complete busts, he'd probably lose his boat. Then he'd probably lose his house. Such a ripple effect touches the non-corporeal as well: spousal relations, child bonds, parental support, self-identity, community, and more. That yoke on his shoulders was why he was distracted when we talked.

Why he pushed us to go faster.

Why he needed us to come through for him.

Why he was well acquainted with boxed wine.

Anthony sat at the table and hummed loudly next to Noah with his dinner, a big-eyed daily reminder of what was at stake for Scott should he fail. I'll admit it, I sort of fell in love with Scott. Not in a romantic way, but in the way that you come to see something for what it is and, at the end of the day, it's simple. It's all about the salmon. It's all about the money. His was a just-keep-swimming existence. Gas prices were high and the last few seasons had been poor. It was the summer of 2008 and the world stood on the precipice of the Great Recession like a would-be euphoric suicide on acid at the edge of the Grand Canyon. We'd have to wait until September 24 to hear President Bush's shaking address to the country, the biggest shock to the American psyche since 9/11: *"...This is an extraordinary period for America's economy. Over the past few weeks, many Americans have felt anxiety over their finances and their future. I understand their worry and their frustration. We've seen triple digit swings in the stock market. Major financial institutions have teetered on the edge of collapse, and some have failed..."*

Perhaps the fishermen already had a hunch. Perhaps we all did.

"At least I'm not like some of the folks around here, hoarding money all their lives," Scott said and ladled thirds and fourths. He had made the suggested serving for three times our number. The pot was scraped clean. Young fishermen eat like bears.

"Every month there is some story about somebody finding a mattress in an abandoned house somewhere full of cash. I swear, the last story I heard, it was one million dollars in cash just sewn up in a mattress in a trailer in the woods. The couple died of old age and lived in poverty their whole lives because they were squirreling away every dollar they earned into that damned mattress. Their whole lives, miserably poor in the woods and sitting on a fortune."

"That's pretty fu—I mean, messed up," Al said. He tried to check his swearing around Anthony whenever Scott was around. When Scott wasn't around, Al didn't care. Scott nodded. The room went quiet for a time. Outside, the night was pitch black. My arrival to Cordova's perpetual twilight of the solstice seemed so long ago. Anthony yawned.

"Time for bed. Come on, bud," Scott said and pinched Anthony's shoulders.

"Can I shoot off a few firecrackers first?" Anthony asked. We didn't get a chance to launch his stash on the Fourth of July. We celebrated with hard work and a fat pay off instead.

"Sure, bud. Go get 'em. We're saving most of them for your birthday next week, remember," Scott said.

Anthony scampered off.

"Now this I gotta see," Noah grinned and followed the crowd onto the deck. I stayed behind and started to wash the dishes. I thought about the hoarders in the woods, so afraid of being poor and how they had lived in isolated wretchedness. Explosions popped from the deck. The crew roared with laughter.

"That one almost blew off your nuts, dad!" Anthony squealed.

I ran to join them.

The next day was our best yet at 71,340 pounds. At twenty-seven cents per pound, that was $19,261.80 for the boat. $1,926.18 of that was mine. My journal for the day reads simply; *More later… I'm tired.*

Scott Brown Jr. got in the habit of staying anchored at Shoup Bay, cancelling Valdez out of the equation and almost guaranteeing first set. On one such day, he invited his friend, the skipper of the *Heathen*, over to help him do "maintenance on the *Solstice*'s engine." I had a feeling a few new boxes of cheap wine would soon be floating on the ocean. Captains' Night, skippers drink free.

We were promptly shepherded onto the skiffs of the *Heathen* and *Mantis* to go ashore for a multi-crew bonfire. Nobody can get a bonfire going on a beach as quickly as Alaskans can and soon a fire was roaring. A skiff man named Nick wrestled with Anthony and talked about hunting. Apparently, he had killed one of the domestic rabbits running around Valdez by throwing a stick and ate it. Anthony was fascinated. The desire to have an animal as a pet and hunt it may stem from the same fascination.

I was content to wander the pebble beach by myself. Shoup Point was in fjord country and emerald swaths of trees coated the mountain flanks around me. Snow clung to the summits and fed glacial streams that cascaded down the slopes like the tears of gods. Tendrils of evening fog slithered over land like great serpents. A sea otter broke the surface of the ocean nearby to look at me, his black doll eyes centered on a furry, whiskered face. He paddled his body half out of the water to better see me before sinking under the green.

What a lot of people don't seem to appreciate about green seawater is that it's green because it is saturated with living things. Productive is the word used by scientists. I call it miraculous. The crystal-clear waters of tropical climes that get all the attention are, by comparison, dead. Sterile. Devoid. It's the cloudy green seas of Earth that are most full of the wonderous offerings; a sacred uterine blood of raw life that includes the smallest and largest lifeforms our planet has ever produced.

I walked past where the otter disappeared and caught a glimpse of him resurface when I glanced over my shoulder. I spun around and waved.

"Hi!" I called. He disappeared under the surface again but followed me while I hiked on shore to peek at me when my back was turned. I came upon a flock of oystercatchers and they scattered with mewling protests. I had stumbled upon a nest. Three speckled eggs sat in the rocks at my feet. Anthony ran to my side.

"Wow, eggs," he pointed and reached down to grab one.

"Leave 'em alone, Anthony," I said. He looked at me as if I was crazy. "You don't want to take these babies from their mamma, do you?" Anthony looked back at the eggs.

"I want to raise one as a pet," Anthony declared and reached for the eggs again. "Or eat it. Hey!" I grabbed his wrist, firmly but gently.

"No Anthony, let them be. The egg probably won't survive if you take it and it belongs here," I said. He squirmed. Anthony didn't take no lightly.

"But I want it!" Anthony argued. He tried to squirm out of my grasp, but I held it tight and moved between him and the nest. He tried to bite me. I held back his face with my other hand.

"Not a good enough reason," I said. "Look around you Anthony. Look at all this beauty. These eggs are part of this perfection, you know? Why ruin it?" I looked at the eggs. A single white feather sat on one of them. Damn, I was working myself up. "It's just not right, give them a chance."

Anthony went limp. I let him go. He tried a final juke past me to the nest, but I picked him up, twirled him around, and set him back down again. He stuck out his tongue and left to destroy something else. An empty box of cheap wine washed up on the beach.

Performance anxiety faded and monotony took hold as we of the *Solstice* graduated from hopelessly green status. Most days of fishing were pretty much the same.

0500 hours, awake.

0600 hours, ready.

Hit the bear trap.

Ready the towline for the throw.

Hit the water with plungers.

Throw the towline.

Fight for life in the seine.

Swear through some kind of fuck up. Somehow they were always different.

Wrestle salmon into the hold.

Go down the hold for the delivery.

Shovel fish.

Make money.

Repeat. Repeat. Repeat.

On July 11, we caught 49,960 pounds, 37,000 pounds of which were from a single epic set. We had to deliver right to the tender from the net again and Scott Brown Jr. was all grins and talking a storm. I knew we had to be making steady progress to $100,000 and black ink when Scott was the talkative one. On this occasion, he was feeling so good that he played music on the deck. We had heard other crews working to music, usually some kind of metal-screamo or vintage rock. Scott Brown Jr. played the Dixie Chicks.

Taaake meee awaaayyy—

"What is this gay-ass shit?" Al grimaced.

—fly this girl as high as you can, and closer to youuu—

"My dad has the same album," I yelled from the deck to Scott. He gave me the thumbs up.

"I love me some Dixie Chicks," Scott hooted. Damn, that was a high. Scott even called me fast that day. I only fell behind once when he gave us the machine's max. I recovered fast enough to keep going.

Quantity wise, the rest of the sets that day were lousy. One was even completely empty. Not one fish. If it weren't for that first set, we would've been as pissed as the rest of the fleet. A closure was predictably announced. We steamed back to Valdez.

Madness and Redemption

Bruised. Dirty. Starved.

I sprinted down mud cliffs, cold wind cutting my lungs as I crashed through undergrowth. My right wrist bled freely down my arm.

How did that happen?

I found the stash of my things in the bush behind the Valdez school where I left it. My cell phone blinked with a new text. It was from Al.

"where r u? we r about to leave." It was 1415 hours.

"Oh no!" I howled and ran, delirious with hunger.

I crossed town in a painful eyeblink and nearly ran into Scott Brown Jr. on the docks. He licked a vanilla soft serve ice cream cone and stepped onto the *Solstice* just as I arrived. Scott drilled me with his icy blues. The announcement of an opener was at noon. We always left at 1400 hours at the latest. He stared at me, expecting something. His words of when he hired me echoed in my head: *Be on time or I'll leave you behind.*

"I'll never do that again," I said numbly.

"Ever," Scott said quietly and entered the wheelhouse. I was empty, devoid of feeling as we cast off and motored back to Shoup. There was no way we were going to be first in line. No way.

"Where the fuck were you, dude?" Al asked. "We were starting to worry."

I decided to hike up the trail Noah and his *Sil-Ver-Fish* friends had showed me, but I pushed beyond. Far beyond. We had been in Valdez for a couple of days during a closer and I figured another closer was going to be announced today at noon. The plan was to go up with the sun and be back in time for the announcement. What could go wrong?

I wanted to be light, so I didn't eat breakfast. I stashed my phone, jacket, and wallet in the bush behind the school and started the climb on all fours up the muddy flank. I pushed myself higher, beyond where the trail began to thin. Bear scat thick with wild blueberry seeds flagged my way.

Faster.

Further.

A pair of woodpeckers dodged around my head and moved like clockwork toys up and down scraggly tree trunks. The forest gave way to tall, wavy grassland. I left Valdez and the constant boat-related responsibilities behind me in the clouds. As I climbed, the soil could not lay claim to the rock and I wheezed over slopes of shale. Shale formed millions of years ago under an ancient faraway subaquatic place. The shrill chirps of pika egged me on. Flocks of white ptarmigans shuffled nervously as I passed. A juvenile bald eagle soared overhead. The pika fell silent. She dove at an adult eagle and they circled each other. They were so close I could've knocked them both out of the sky with a baseball bat.

I kept up the suicide pace, goaded by some instinct within me. Scuba divers beware a buildup of excess nitrogen in their bloodstreams or risk a condition called nitrogen narcosis. The effects on the diver are like intoxication and stories abound of divers blissfully swimming toward the dark blue abyss and their deaths. Perhaps I was consumed by some similar elemental buildup in my brain.

I climbed until I couldn't anymore and collapsed to the ground on a bed of crusty summer snow at the top of a high peak. A trio of fine-looking ravens did not regard me with any fear nor interest as they held their meeting. I sat among them peacefully. My summit was surrounded by clouds and the only visible sight was the next peak a few hundred feet higher along the ridge. There was probably a higher peak beyond. Then another one. There were so many mountains around there that I imagine they enjoyed dignified names like Peak #1204A by the United States Geological Survey.

Thirst struck. I sucked on snow. I was exactly the kind of young person who dies on these kinds of hikes. The type of poorly planned mission people read about in the paper under the headline *Dead Dummy Found in Park X*. The average reader shakes his or her head at such stories, suddenly an outdoor expert.

"That idiot got what was coming to him," is the typical mantra of Professor Survival as he yanks the lever on his recliner armchair to pop up his bunioned feet. He usually reaches for a bag of pork rinds and a Pabst tallboy before diving into a long yarn about that one time, decades ago, when he broke a sweat. I can't speak for Chris McCandless of *Into the Wild* notoriety, but I certainly wasn't asking for it. Dammit, I was alive on peak number whatever in the clouds and wanted to stay that way.

Sometimes you don't need a watch to know you're pushing the clock. I forced myself to my feet and jogged down the way I came. I became less euphoric and more panicked with each step as I left the pika cries and snow behind. I tore through the grass and stepped on a fresh pile of bear scat. I tumbled through the bush, trail lost but direction clear.

Down, you moron, get down!

A branch took off the skin of my wrist like a cheese grater. I slid on the mud and messed up my shins. My empty stomach yelled for mercy. I shoveled wild blueberries and fiddleheads down my gullet without pause. If I had stumbled upon another ptarmigan, I would have wrung its neck and eaten it raw. The clouds burned away and gorgeous Valdez stretched out below.

I made the final punishing push to my stash behind the school.

"Damn man, I just got turned around up there. I'm sorry, guys," I said as I attacked a sandwich, nearly faint. Al shrugged and started up Guitar Hero.

We ended up seventh in line. It was an ok day, about 20,000 pounds total. The *Mantis* was first in line and they caught the 10,000 extra pounds the first set usually yielded. The floodlights from the tender were blinding when we delivered that night, but Scott's blues shone upon me the brightest. I offered a nervous smile, but I knew what he was telling me. He didn't need to say a damned word.

You cost me 10,000 pounds, buddy.

I never want anybody to look at me that way again. Fortunately, feelings weren't hard with the crew. We stayed up too late and got silly with Anthony. He got his hands on some kind of filtration sack with black carbon beanies in them.

"They're bunny food, Anthony," Noah said.

"Really? Are they good? I'm going to eat them," Anthony said and started to shovel the black things into his mouth.

"Anthony, no! He could die—" I started. Noah's eyes glowed with a mad gleam that terrified us all.

"Yes. Yes, he might!" Noah cackled hopefully. We all lost it and laughed. Anthony hardly knew what a dinosaur was outside the context of the creationist's Noah's Ark, much to my horror. I cracked open my journal and drew to-scale sketches of a Tyrannosaurus, Triceratops, and Brachiosaurus and talked about the Mesozoic Era they were from. Scott Brown Jr. was upstairs, probably hitting the boxed wine.

"I wish I had a book like that," Anthony said quietly as I drew in my leather-bound journal. His birthday was soon. I finally knew what to get him.

The hours grew long and we shuffled to bed. I had the salmon dream again, the one where the fish all had people faces. I woke up in a cold sweat and didn't quite fall back asleep.

All I could hear was the groan of the power block and the slap of my hands on the lead line. I hunched forward, my orange work gloves and the growing pile of black webbing at my feet my entire world. A piece of seaweed bounced off my jacket hood.

I glanced forward. Scott's lips were drawn tight, his eyes invisible behind dark sunglasses on a cloudy day. My eyes darted to Al before I doubled down on the work. Al's cork piles grew like soft serve ice cream out of the spigot. Perfect.

Whomp! A clusterfuck of lead line landed on the deck. Good thing we weren't working directly underneath the power block like rookies. Just another day in the office.

I huffed. There was still a while to go on the set. My mind emptied and my body reduced to its essence, a twitching sack of nerves and muscle. The power block slowed to a crawl. I straightened to see what was happening, fearing mechanical trouble. Scott's jaw was slack.

What gives?

"Holy shit," Al's voice carried over the growling power block. "Holy *shit!*" He was looking into the seine. The block inched to a stop.

"What?" I asked. The salmon answered as they broke the surface in a thunder of fins. I stumbled over to Al, lead line forgotten. Scott joined us, our hands white on the rail. The salmon churned the sea into a furious rapid of silver and white.

"*Yeeehawww!*" Scott Brown Jr. howled over the deafening splashes. The boat groaned and heeled under the strength of the panicked school. Al and I punched each other on the shoulders until we bruised. A carnivorous smile spread over Scott's face. The Dixie Chicks blasted over the deck.

"I'm calling in the tender. We're delivering right out of the net," Scott declared and another *yeehaw* escaped him. Al and I swore and laughed, filled with uncensored joy. Meanwhile, the boats after us in line didn't get anything to write home about. We had grabbed the pot of gold, fair and square, and held the school in the embrace of our seine until the tender arrived. The tender inserted its proboscis and sucked up our haul without a hitch. We gathered around Scott to hear the final count.

"55,000 pounds," Scott howled and motored back to the lineup. Miraculously, we made it back to the line just in time to take our turn. I hit the bear trap and Noah was off again. And wouldn't you know it, but our luck was almost as good the second set. And the third.

The radio chatter among the rest of the fleet was baffled and envious, for if we were doing anything different from the rest, Scott kept it a secret. Al and I were deckhand gods, chomping at the bit to suck the ocean dry. We threw aside the hatch boards to the hold. Scott loaded another handsome set that tumbled into the cold water with thuds and silent screams. The working deck writhed with spilled fish to be pitched. Al went aft to secure Noah and the skiff. I set about picking fish from the deck, a salmon in each hand. Scott's smile was so big and goofy he looked like a different person.

At the end of the day, we delivered 97,090 pounds, a pittance shy of a Hundy—100,000 pounds—something Scott Brown Jr. said he never accomplished before. Of course, we announced to the world that we made it. We'd wipe our ass with 2,010 pounds, the missing ton. The *Solstice*'s Hundy was a miracle, nobody in Shoup caught anything close to that. Scott even called it the single best day of his entire fishing career. Our eyes met again under the floodlights of the tender when we delivered late in the night. He nodded once, a satisfied smirk on the edge of his mouth. It was the highest compliment I'll ever receive.

Shoup Bay N' Back (N' Out Again)

Scott Brown Jr. didn't go to Valdez anymore during closers. Perhaps it was my doing for being late on my hike to the heavens, a breach of trust he hadn't quite shaken. I preferred to think Scott thought we sat on another Hundy and wanted to be extra sure we were first in the lineup. Perhaps both. Regardless, Al, Noah, and I were confined to the *Solstice* during closers with little to do. Our movie selection, nothing to boast of in the first place, grew tired. Pokémon on Anthony's Gameboy Advance or Guitar Hero on the Wii just wasn't going to cut it anymore. The weather was rainy enough so one might've thought we were back in Cordova. "Cooped up" and "cabin fever" were cute ways of saying a few of us were devolving into insanity. Al especially had a tough time. He paced in the cabin.

"This is gay, why aren't we in Valdez?" Al fumed aloud every few minutes. Noah plugged away at Pokémon, his brow furrowed and thumbs tapping. I wrote in my journal.

"Gay-ass shit, man. Gay-ass *shit*. Let's just go," Al half begged. Noah and I were quiet with our amusements, not biting the hook.

"Seriously, we can just hike there. There's the trail on the ridge that goes right into town." Noah threw up his hands, sighed, and turned off the

Gameboy with the disdain of a five-star chef discarding a sub-par tomato. He rubbed his eyes.

"Yeah, I agree. I'm going crazy. Let's go, we can take the trail," Noah said. The two schemed while I enjoyed the warmth of the cabin and the comfort of my journal. I glanced outside. Fat raindrops and insidious fog were about all I needed to convince me to stay, but I listened in on their plot. They were to hike to Valdez along a trail they were familiar with and crash the *Sil-Ver-Fish* that was still in town for repairs. Then they were going to catch a ride back to Shoup with Al's dad on the *Carmen Lilly* in the morning.

"What would we do in town?" I asked.

"We could do laundry, take a shower..." Noah's exciting list ended there.

"We could do *something* man. This is so gay and that little shit—" Al whispered shit and pointed up to where Anthony was in the wheelhouse. The two had a row over the Gameboy earlier. "—is driving me crazy. You in man?" I looked to Noah. He was already packing.

"I dunno," I said.

"Well think fast. I'm talking to Scott," Al said and was up the ladder. I didn't think Scott would be ok with the plan, but Al emerged with a smile a few minutes later.

"We're getting outta here. Scott's dropping us off at the beach. You in?"

I paused on the edge of a precipice.

I jumped.

"Aw, what the hell, sure," I said. We stuffed our laundry into a red duffel bag and each tended to our own backpacks before Scott dropped us off near Shoup Point with the skiff. He summed up my opinion perfectly.

"This is kind of a bad idea," was all he said, *kind of* being the real crux of the matter. Good or bad was too strong of an opinion for this plan. *Kind of bad* was pragmatic and took off the edge of *bad idea*. If pulling a tiger's tail is a *bad idea*, then approaching the tiger's den in the first place was a *kind of bad* idea. Neither are great choices.

Scott motored back to the *Solstice* and we were left on shore in our raingear and boots. It was early afternoon, but clouds choked the sunlight to create a brooding mood. The place was just so grey, like the rain had blended all the colors into a dreary, muddy shadow. This was, in essence, the kind of weather ripe for nasty things to happen. My two companions charged into the bush with gusto, hell bent on running the whole way. They had done the trail once in warm, dry weather. Conditions were quite the opposite.

"The trail is right up here, stop asking," Al snapped at my inquiry. The cliffs were so muddy we could've been ants climbing a chocolate cake as we bullied our way at a mad pace, Noah and Al rabid to shake off cabin fever. I eyed the heights we climbed and wished we slowed down. Noah fell and tumbled a good way. He clutched his knee and rubbed a bleeding cut on the bridge of his nose. Al and I helped him to his feet.

"Guys, running is really dumb," I said.

"Ok, Oregon," Al said Oregon like it was a swear. My ears grew red, but I kept it together. We ran a little further before Al ate it in the mud as well. He just about fell back onto us.

"Nice one, Alaska," I retorted. We stopped running and soon found the trail. We made swift progress after moderating our pace to that of a light jog. The sound of rushing water drew nearer. Sure enough, the trail curved along a whitewater ride maybe fifteen or more feet wide. The trail turned inland and followed the river upstream. I kept my eyes peeled for a bridge, but we were led to the riverbank instead. This patch of the river wasn't white, I reckoned because it was deeper. A sandbar sat a short distance from the bank.

"Wow, this river is deeper than before," Noah said and tromped into the current toward the sandbar. The water wasn't quite up to his knees. He ended up on the sandbar easily.

"Yup," Al said and tromped after him. I hesitated, but the walk to the sandbar didn't intimidate me. What lay beyond did though. Twenty or so feet of deep running water waited for us. We all paused on the sandbar.

"Wait, we're not just walking through, are we?" I asked. They looked ahead and didn't meet my eyes. "Wait, are you kidding me?"

"It's not a big deal," Al said.

"Hey, I may be from Oregon, but we have rivers down there. People get taken away in rivers like this all the time."

"Fine! Fuckin' turn back then," Al snapped. We stared off for a few seconds before Noah took the first step. Al was second. I took a deep breath, lifted the red duffel bag of laundry above my head, and followed. The tribe had spoken. We were the crew of the *Solstice*.

The glacier water stung in an uncomfortably erotic fashion, and we didn't take more than a few steps before we were in over our hips. Our line couldn't maintain a straight course and we began to bend downriver. Noah's arms flailed as he lost his footing. I sure as hell was losing my feet, especially with my hands over my head with the duffel. I slid on the algae slime that coated the river's smooth stones. I tried not to think of the waterfalls downstream.

Noah pitched forward and, swimming, managed to grab the branches of an overhanging tree. He pulled himself to shore. Al grabbed the limbs in the nick of time too. I threw him the duffel and half swam my way to the tree and safety. We panted on the bank and tipped water out of our boots.

I don't remember them calling me Oregon again.

The trail leveled and we ran into town on boardwalks over the marsh Valdez was built upon. Al peeled off to find his dad while Noah and I made our way to the familiar Laundromat by the marina. Sadly, the vending machine was out of soaps. I cursed myself for not taking advantage of my black-market connection, Anthony. Noah had an idea and we ended up at a nearby trailer park.

"There are washing machines here," Noah assured me as we walked into the reception shack. I pointed at a warning poster pinned to a bulletin board above the rack of brochures. It warned against crossing the river on the trail after a heavy rain. Noah didn't want to talk about it.

We heard the thumping of laundry machines in the adjacent room, but a large woman with thick glasses barred our way. She gave us a once over. I tried not to stare at the large mole on her upper lip.

"We're full," she said.

"We're not staying here, we just want to pay for some laundry and get some soap," I said and held up our laundry duffel as proof.

"Machines are full," she repeated and that was the end of our conversation. I couldn't decide if she was lying to us or not, but she clearly didn't want us to stay any longer. Noah and I said goodbye politely and hated her as we walked through the rain. To be turned away by a trailer park seemed a bit low.

We returned to the marina Laundromat where we decided to wash our load without soap. Noah went to find the *Sil-Ver-Fish*, our berth for the night, and I planned to take a luxurious four-dollar shower. I was short on clothes, so I wrapped a towel after putting my last pairs of pants and boxers in the machine. My intention was to nip across the street to the shower and back before anybody was aware I wasn't wearing any pants. I power-walked across the street and collected glances from the few people who walked in the rain. I marched up to the harbormaster's office to purchase a shower token and encountered a locked door.

I paused and tried again, incredulous.

They were closed.

No shower for me.

Defeated and pantless, I walked back through the drizzle to the Laundromat and spent the last of my quarters to put our load into the drying machine. I spent a good hour wishing ill to whoever's task it was to restock soaps, the trailer park lady, and the harbormaster. You know, the people who mattered most in my life.

The machine stopped and I reached into our load to put on a pair of sport shorts. They were still wet, not quite dripping, but more than damp. I reached for more quarters and winced. No more. I turned to the change machine. It was out of order. No more drying for us. A cold, wet night gripped the town before Noah rejoined me in the Laundromat. I tried to read his face. He spoke extra quickly.

"So the *Sil-Ver-Fish* isn't here. I'm calling James and Hunter to see if we can crash the *Rikki-Tikki-T*. I saw it in the marina. They haven't answered."

"Our clothes are still wet. Do you have any quarters?" I asked.

"No," Noah said. We looked at the miserable night outside the Laundromat and silently agreed to hunker down. Noah stretched out on a row of washing machines. I lay on top of a table.

"Do you know where Al is?" I asked. I was a step shy of shivering in my wet cotton hoodie and sport shorts.

"Not a clue. He won't respond to my texts," Noah mumbled, his eyes covered under the crook of his elbow.

"Sounds about right," I muttered. Noah sniggered. I closed my eyes, resigned to a rough night. Twenty minutes passed before Noah leapt off the washing machines, his face excited under the illumination of his open cell phone.

"It's James," Noah said. "Let's go to the *Rikki-Tikki-T*!" He didn't have to tell me twice. We scurried to the harbor and entered the cabin of the *Rikki-Tikki-T*. James and Hunter were in their bunks in the v-berth under the glow of a cabin light.

"Long time, no see. Hey James. Hunter," I greeted them.

"Hey bro, welcome aboard," Hunter beckoned to empty berths.

"Thanks guys," Noah said wearily as we got comfortable. There weren't any spare blankets, so I lay on my back and stuffed my hands in my armpits to fight off shivering. At least it was better than the Laundromat.

"You guys were sleeping in the Laundromat? What the hell," James laughed at us. I was past conversational and started to drift off. The Alaskans slid into small town gossip, namely the cute girls.

"I'm telling you man, Jessica blew me at her dad's place," James claimed.

"Bull. Shit!" Hunter contended.

"Dude, I swear, man." And so forth. James had a mouthful to say about the sexual orientation of his skipper, Edmond Wood. Turns out he was gay.

"Dude, I don't know if I should take a nap alone with him around. You know what I mean? What if he pulls some queer-ass shit on me when I'm asleep, you know?"

The summer of 2008 was a different time in many ways, notably LGBTQ+ acceptance in America. Even the term, LGBTQ+ was LGBT and not terribly mainstream. As far as I know, the Q+—for queer and more— was added later as a sort of exclamation point. Even the most liberal circles I knew in Portland thought nationwide, legalized same-sex marriage was a utopian fantasy more than a pragmatic goal. If I used a time machine to tell the people of 2008 about the 2013 Supreme Court case *United States v. Windsor*, they'd have pegged me a liberal agitator or conservative troll.

I cracked my eyes open when Al joined us.

"Heyyy muthafuckahs," Al giggled.

"You're high as balls, aren't you?" Noah asked.

"You fuck'n know it, broheim," Al joined us. The others laughed. He one upped James' raunchy stories and really had 'em going. I fell asleep somehow.

The next morning was a real scramble. Not only was an opener for the following day announced, but Al's dad had left without us. We would've been forced to take the trail back if not for the kindness of the skipper of the seiner

Red Herring, who agreed to drop us off on the *Solstice*. I sat in the wheelhouse with the helmsman Davis, a young man with tattoos covering his arms and the gravelly voice of a heavy smoker. A quiet woman named Marta of similar age and tattoo persuasion was curled in a seat for the ride. She hardly said a word, but Davis and I chatted the whole way, mostly pulling things out of our butts about the season.

We approached Shoup Bay and the seiner *Praetorian* was tied alongside the *Solstice*. It was widely known that Scott Brown Jr. and the *Praetorian*'s skipper, Maggie, were friendly with each other.

"Are those two banging?" Davis asked. Marta sniggered. "They sure are cuddly on the radio." I shrugged. I knew Scott Brown Jr. was unhappily married to Anthony's mom, but rumors persisted.

"Probably?" I offered. Davis nodded and pulled a crack pipe from one of his cargo pockets. He handed it to Marta. She clutched it to her chest as delicately as if it were a baby bird.

Noah, Al, and I tiptoed to the *Solstice*'s cabin door to peer in the window. I can only speak for myself, but I was hoping to see something sordid. Mind you, I was eighteen and keyed up on a boat with a boozing sea captain who commanded my fear and respect, his eleven-year-old bouncy ball, and two high schoolers who were as pent up as I was. I wouldn't be surprised if all three of us had semi-boners as we clustered around the window. I don't remember. Or choose not to reflect too closely.

We looked upon an idyllic scene. Scott and Maggie sat next to each other at the table and played Scrabble. He wore his faded green cap, she a newer navy blue one. Maggie was the kind of fit, ready-for-anything woman usually found in beat up jeans and hoodies. Her brown hair was tied into a ponytail, her eyes bright and a smile quick on her thin lips. She was a ski coach during the off season. If the dream woman of an Alaskan manly man like Scott was a cake, she was the recipe.

We entered the cabin, miffed that playing Scrabble was what the kids were doing these days.

"You guys made it," Scott greeted us. He glanced at the Scrabble board. "Magus is definitely not a word, ya cheat."

"Oh please, look it up. Hello," Maggie said. We murmured hellos and shuffled bashfully into the v-berth. But the cabin was only so big and Maggie seemed to want to talk to us. Scott, visibly annoyed at our return, put the board game away. "How'd it go?" she asked.

"Well," I thought of the muddy hike, the nearly botched river crossing, walking pantless in the streets, sleeping in the Laundromat, shivering aboard the *Rikki-Tikki-T*, the panic at nearly being stranded by Al's dad, and Marta's crack pipe. I smiled, "Great. Did we miss anything here in Shoup?"

"Not the opener tomorrow," Scott growled. A gentle smile played on the edges of Maggie's lips.

"I better go see what my crew is doing," Maggie said and rose to her feet. The two of them exchanged a tender, playful glance.

"See ya soon?" Scott half-asked.

"You could talk me into it," she said. Her voice dropped an intimate octave. "Lucky for you, you're better at more important things than Scrabble." Blushing and uncomfortably aroused, I excused myself and went out onto the deck to get to some air. The sun made its first appearance in days. I soaked it in and appreciated the scenery.

Good to be back.

"Not a bad view, huh?" I started at the female voice. A girl my age stood on the deck of the *Praetorian*. Her flashing green eyes hit me like a bouquet of thrown flowers.

"Doesn't get much better," I agreed. We walked toward each other. "I'm Norris."

"Genevieve. You a deckhand?" Genevieve asked. Her hair was in a ponytail that played in the breeze and she tucked a loose lock of blonde hair behind an ear. Like her skipper, she wore a hoodie with old jeans and looked ready for just about anything.

"Yup, first season," I said.

"Me too," Genevieve smiled. Man, did she *smile*.

"How'd you get into all this?" I gestured around us.

"Maggie is my ski coach and she offered me the gig. What about you?" Genevieve asked. I thought for a few seconds and laughed.

"You know, I'm still trying to figure that out. I'm from Oregon and it just sort of... happened," I said.

"You're from Oregon? I'm going to Oregon for college," she said.

"Really? Where?" I asked.

"Lewis and Clark. Do you know it?"

"Know it? They have a campus right by my family's house," I said. Genevieve and I leaned over the rails of our boats to talk face-to-face.

"No way! That's crazy," she said. Maggie emerged onto the deck. The skipper glanced at us knowingly and stepped aboard the *Praetorian*.

"Dinner ready?" Maggie asked.

"Yeah, I think Evan is just about done," Genevieve said.

"Evan is cooking? Oh lordy," Maggie sighed and entered the *Praetorian*'s cabin. Genevieve turned to me. Her ponytail danced behind her.

"I better get in there before there isn't any food left. See you later?" She half-asked.

Dear lord, I hope so. I gestured to the deck of the *Solstice*.

"You know where to find me," I said. Genevieve followed her skipper inside. I turned to the mountains and grinned like a buffoon.

Al, Noah, and I were on deck between sets on another rainy July opener. Noah sat on the bow of the skiff like he was born in it. Al and I lounged on the seine like we pissed on it. We owned the place. The other boats in the lineup floated in the grey around us.

"I mean, the count is seventy percent female," Noah said in his fast mumble. "This run is almost up. We haven't caught much recently."

"You kidding me? What about the fuckin' Hundy, man?" Al objected. I offered him a high five and he slapped it.

"Hun-*dy!*" We hooted. Al popped a Fireball candy.

"Seventy percent female? What does that mean?" I asked.

"The more females, the closer the run is to ending," Noah explained. We already set first in the lineup and caught next to nothing. I was getting the feeling that the Hundys were over. Scott Brown Jr. emerged from the wheelhouse and stood above us at the top of the ladder.

"Yeah, there isn't much left in this run—*whoa*," Scott stumbled and caught the rail. Good thing too because he would've taken a nasty tumble onto the deck otherwise. His face was bright red when he recovered, his eyes glassed over. Al and I exchanged a glance. "I don't know what you all are doing when we're back in Cordova, but I'll pay ya fifteen an hour to help me with a few of my house projects."

$15 an hour, eh?

Our crew shares for the season so far pushed $10k, not bad for about a month of work. Not only that, but when people talked about the boats that were doing well, the *Solstice* always came up, a true highliner for the season. The Valdez run hadn't been kind to most of the fleet.

"Get ready," Scott told us and disappeared back into the wheelhouse to set us up off the beach. I sauntered over to the bear trap. Noah positioned himself behind the skiff console. Al cleared the way for the seine to go out. We all gave each other stern, manly looks.

High. Liners.

"Go!" Scott yelled. I hit the bear trap. Noah peeled out and we deckhands did the routine. I flaked the towline and Al hosed off the deck.

"What are you going to do when we get back to Cordova?" I asked as I placed my coiled towline in position, port amidships. Al moseyed across the work deck after the seine was fully deployed and soaking. He arced the hose water in lazy wreaths.

"I don't know, man. I'm going to be bored as hell, probably," Al said. He hosed a cluster of old jellies overboard. The seine set for the usual time and Scott ordered Noah to close it up. I got ready with the towline as Noah turned the skiff for the return to the *Solstice*.

The skiff lurched. Noah was pitched onto the skiff console.

"What the hell?" Al put a hand over his eyes to block out the sun burning through the fog. Noah was caught on something.

"He caught a rock," Scott growled.

"A rock," I echoed. Scott hustled to the radio in the wheelhouse.

"Double back, Noah. Noah? Noah! Double back!" Scott yelled over the radio. "Fuckin' thing," Scott cursed and slammed down the receiver. He rejoined us on the deck. "Go! Back!" Scott yelled over the water and waved his arms. Poor Noah's head snapped back and forth like a frightened gopher. He turned the wheel this way and that, but the skiff remained snagged.

As a deckhand, I was used to sweating in jellyfish while the skiffman lounged on his seat, a smug little skipper who didn't have to get his hands too dirty. I wanted to be the skiffman ninety percent of the time. But you couldn't pay me to be the skiffman for that other ten percent.

Noah tried to double back.

"Don't use reverse! I hate it when he does that," Scott growled. My hands clenched. Al and I were completely helpless. We watched Noah try in vain to untangle the seine, but it was for not. The lineup wasn't going to put up with this for much longer.

High... Liners?

The radio buzzed with Noah's panicked voice. Scott lumbered up the ladder. Al and I exchanged a glance.

"Unclip it, Noah. Noah. Noah! *Unclip* it, we're pulling the seine in!" Scott yelled.

Crap, we lost the set.

Al and I got into position. If we hauled the seine in fast enough, maybe we could still claim our second set. Noah unclipped the gear and motored back to us. I threw him the towline.

Clunk!

Bull's eye. Toad in the hole. Egg in the muthafuckin' basket.

Scott blasted the power block. Al and I had the seine on deck and ready to go in no time. Noah was silent after we secured the skiff. He didn't look up from a line he fiddled with.

"Don't worry about it man, not your fault," I said. He glanced at me with a frown.

"Second set. Get ready!" Scott yelled. Noah jumped into action. Al hit the bear trap. We were off again. Scott joined us on deck as the seine went out.

"We're doing this for Noah. I don't want him to feel bad," Scott said. Al and I understood. A confident skiffman was a good skiffman. Noah hugged the beach like he had a hundred times at Shoup to let the seine soak. Scott gave the order. Noah turned to close the seine. The skiff lurched again.

Noah was caught on the same rock.

"Fuck!" Al swore.

"Fuck," I echoed.

96

"Back around!" Scott yelled over the water and waved his hands. Noah tried. "He needs to not use the reverse," Scott hissed. We weren't getting free. Scott got on the radio.

"Noah, unclip!" He yelled. Al and I wound up on the deck, ready to deploy our brawn somewhere. Anywhere. Noah unclipped and returned to the *Solstice*. I threw him the towline.

Clunk!

...egg in the muthafuckin' basket—

"What the fuck!" Scott howled. The seine wasn't coming loose of the rock this time, despite the power block's efforts. We were reeling ourselves to shore on the snagged gear.

"Ummm?" Al hummed and eyed the approaching land. Noah's towing wasn't helping either. Scott killed the power block a few boat lengths away from the beach.

"Noah, tow us away from shore!" Scott yelled. Noah was frazzled, his eyes wide as he worked the wheel and throttle of the console.

"Away-!"

DUHNN-rk! The *Solstice* pitched like a whale rammed her. I caught my fall with a foot, Al by flailing his arms. Scott flopped onto the deck winch and stayed bent over like he lost his wind.

"Holy shit!" Al yelled and ran to the side of the boat. "We're aground."

"Mother*fucker!*" Scott swore and scrambled up to the wheelhouse. He gunned the engine. An abrasive grinding sound made me cringe.

"He is going to wreck the prop," Al lamented. I entered a beast's survival state where anything to do with the brain was shut off. I was a ball of reflexes that yearned to fix the problem by following orders and pulling on something.

"Fuck!" Scott shouted as he almost fell down the ladder onto the deck again. He caught the rail and stumbled back into the wheelhouse, his face bright red. The skiffman of another seiner *Churriana* came to our rescue, a venerable seaman with a grey beard. We threw the new skiffman a line while he coordinated Noah into position. The two skiffs went full power and the *Solstice* was freed from the shallows, her tail tucked between her legs. We thanked the *Churriana* skiffman and the unsung hero left to return to his job.

The day was a complete embarrassment. The rock was named Scott Rock by the fleet and for all I know they still call it that. Scott said we had to go back to Cordova to repair or replace the prop, patch the seine, check the hull, hope people forgot what they saw, and who knows what else.

So ended our Valdez run as highline fuck ups. Not one of us blamed Noah, our poor skiffman. Murphy's Law abides. We comforted ourselves by repeating things like, "Seventy percent females? *Pffft*, the season is dead anyway!" To make defeat a bit easier to swallow, Scott rafted us up with the *Praetorian* for the night.

"I just want you guys to know that I'm sorry for messing up today and yelling. Today's giant fuck up was my fault. I'm sorry," said Scott. He hung his head before he disappeared to the comfort of Maggie's wheelhouse for the night. Accepting an apology from the skip was an uncomfortable experience for me, but we got cozy in the *Solstice* cabin. Al's fingers were a blur on the Wii guitar as Noah and I chatted. We scraped our plates clean of Hamburger Helper made with moose burger that Noah cooked.

"You know what, Noah? I think we've made more money than the other deckhands I've talked to. I think we're over ten grand," I said.

"Yeah… we'd have even more if I didn't mess up," Noah grimaced.

"Hey man, the run is seventy percent females. *Pffft*, the season is dead anyway!" I said for maybe the seventh time.

"Today was bullshit," Al mumbled, his eyes fixed on the screen.

"Yeah, bullshit," I echoed.

"Yeah," Noah said and looked at his twiddling thumbs. The door to the cabin opened. My heart skipped a beat when Genevieve walked inside. We all snapped straight at attention.

"Hey guys. Rough day, huh?" Genevieve said with a friendly, confident smile.

"You have no idea," I sighed. Al practically threw the Wii guitar aside and stood up as tall as he could. He jammed his hands in his pockets and gave her a chin-up head nod.

"Sup," Al said. She raised an amused brow.

"Anybody sitting here?" Genevieve pointed to the empty space across the table from me.

"Nope," I said. She sat down and leaned forward.

"Sooo... what exactly happened?" She asked. I told the story with Al and Noah commentary. Genevieve laughed at us, which felt good for some reason. Anthony scrambled down from the wheelhouse.

"You little monster, get over here," Genevieve reached for him and tickled his ribs. Anthony rolled into a protective cackling ball. "What now, little man?" She challenged him. Anthony doubled up and punched her in the chest. Genevieve recoiled and Anthony wiggled free. "You punched me in the boob, little man. Off limits!"

"Nyah nyah!" Anthony stuck out his tongue and escaped up the ladder to the wheelhouse. The rest of us chatted into the night about all kinds of things. She wanted to know about Oregon because she was heading down there to college soon.

We even talked a little about politics. She was a fan of Obama, the hopeful new black presidential candidate who shocked the country by defeating Hillary Clinton in the Democratic Primaries. In true American mythos fashion, the primary race echoed the year's Kentucky Derby when the legendary filly Eight Belles made her stand among the colts. She ran a hard race but suffered compound fractures of both front ankles and was put down on the track as per the sport's ancient way. The horse Big Brown took the race. Cosmic humor at work.

The night matured and talk turned to more personal matters, things like dreams we've had and what we wanted out of our lives. Genevieve and I melted onto our seats until we lay on our bellies, our heads cradled in our folded arms. We talked to each other under the table and caught each other's eyes when we thought the other wasn't looking. Early morning was upon us when Genevieve dismissed herself with a yawn.

"Goodnight," Genevieve said softly as she walked out of the cabin. "Some of us who aren't deadbeats have to fish in the morning."

"Good luck. If you mess up, we'll be sure to stay clear of Maggie Rock," I said.

"Ha! Not going to happen. See you later," she said as she closed the door. The three of us let loose a collective sigh and prepared for sleep.

"Dude, I'd totally bang the shit out of her," Al said.

"Would you now?" I asked and started to brush my teeth.

"She's hot as ballz, man," Al said.

Got me there, I thought.

I went to bed with a dumb smile on my face. Al and Noah were in a philosophical mood and muttered in the dark. Al thought life was supposed to be lived to the fullest, a big party. Noah was pessimistic about the collective mindset of society and wished to be left to his own resourcefulness. It was a bit like listening to a conversation between Evil Knievel and Ayn Rand.

I wrote in my journal that I couldn't wait to cross paths with Genevieve again, but I never got the chance. She banged up her knee or something and called the season off early. Flew back home and got ready for college. When I heard the news through the fleet's grapevine several days too late, I felt like a salmon in the seine, caught up by something big that didn't care one lick about me or what I wanted. I was just a piece of marketplace meat worth twenty-seven cents a pound.

Cordova, Again

I marched through the Cordova drizzle and up the hill to Hawk House with a spring in my step and a red duffle of dirty laundry over my shoulder. Sophie's yipping echoed my knock on the door. It opened and Larry stood in the entranceway.

"Norris. Come on in, my boy," Larry ushered me in with a big grin. "Sisään!" he commanded in Finnish.

"Ahoy, Larry!" I smiled and put down my duffel. I scarcely removed my shoes before he put me to work in the kitchen. His Eastern European aristocrat aura was enhanced by his silver mustache and a small branch of varicose veins on his big ruddy nose.

"The dinner hour approaches and there is much to do. You're on salad duty," Larry declared and placed me in front of packages of spinach and a pile of freshly cut bell peppers. He spun around to tend to his masterpiece, a deep-dish creation of noodles, olives, onions, locally hunted mushrooms, and bison burger. Pete the gossip ventured into the kitchen and his roaming bloodhound eyes studied me. He hovered at the edge of the action with one hand in his pocket and a glass of water in the other.

"Welcome back, Moneybags," Pete smiled sheepishly. The *Solstice's* success was no secret. I don't think there were any secrets in that small town. I threw all the veggies into the bowl.

"Hey Pete," I greeted him while I tossed the salad. Larry watched my technique out of the corner of his critical eye while he poured olive oil into a small bowl. He was making balsamic vinaigrette dressing.

"You know, I saw Scott Brown Jr. today by the docks," Pete hung the statement in the air. I held my breath. "I asked him about you."

I dropped the salad thongs into the sink.

"Oh yeah?" I stuttered and picked up the clattering thongs.

"Yup. I asked, 'So, how's Norris doing?' Scott says, 'Fine.' Then I says, 'So, I hear you had an all green crew this year.' Scott says, 'They're not green anymore.' And then he turns and walks away. Like always, man of many words. He is a strange fellow," Pete said. I laughed, the scene clear in my head.

"That's sounds about right. Strange indeed," I said. I thought of the many conversations with Scott in the wheelhouse doomed from the get-go and left in the air to die. I also reckoned Anthony could make a decent fort out of the empty boxes of wine Scott left in his wake. The hiss of an opened beer interrupted my reflections.

"Who wants one? Norris? Want a beer?" Larry offered.

"He's underage," Pete reminded Larry curtly.

"Bah! When I was Norris' age, I was stoned out of my mind most of the time. Want one, Norris?" Larry asked. I looked at the two of them and felt Pete's disappointment in my answer.

"Sure!" I said. Larry popped the cap off an Alaskan Pale Amber and handed it to me. I paused to study the bottle. A fishing vessel underway fatefully graced the label. Larry took a sip and looked at me with a cocked brow. "Something wrong?" He put his lips to his bottle for another drink.

"It's just… I've never had a beer before… you know, outside the family," I said. Larry choked and almost sprayed a mouthful of the stuff on me. He managed to swallow and wiped his mouth with the back of his hand.

"You're not serving up a load of bull now, are you?" Larry asked with a scowl.

"No, sir!" I stammered and took a deep swig. I wasn't a fan, it tasted kind of like carbonated, bitter bread. I wasn't sure what all the fuss was about. Larry's deep-dish creation was ready, so we moved to the table and dug in. Red wine appeared and jazz music began to play, a combination I learned the Hawk House Intellectuals magically summoned at whim. Fish talk dominated conversation as we got comfortable. They had a hoot about the Scott Rock story.

"So the skiffman from the *Churriana* came up and passed us a rope—"

"Line," Larry interrupted. I started. He shook his head and dug into his food with a knife and fork. "There is no idle *rope* on a boat, Norris. Only working *line*." The two fishermen had plenty of nautical knowledge to share. I tried to remember things to note in my journal.

"So, big tide is the highest tide. Up tide is any tide higher than a zero-low tide, and a zero-low tide is a low tide, while a minus tide is below the zero-low mark," Pete explained as I scratched my head. Conversation didn't stay on fishing forever and as the beer bottles emptied and empty glasses of wine refilled, talk turned to sports, music, celebrities, world issues, and politics. The Hawk House Intellectuals really started to earn their namesake. The Beijing Summer Olympics was coming up and there wasn't much love for China's trade policies or human rights record around the table. Larry insisted that the Bush Administration was driving America off a cliff. He thumped his hand on the table.

"They ought to hand Cheney over to me and I'll waterboard the fascist myself," he announced. Pete was more reserved, his eyes shifting as if the wrong person may be listening. Dora returned home as we cleaned our plates, her formal business skirt and jacket odd sights in Cordova.

"Look who's back," Pete nodded to me. I waved. A smile spread across her face as she recognized me.

"Welcome home," Dora said and joined us until it was time to go to bed.

The adults occupied the rooms upstairs and I was informed that there was space for me in the basement. I promptly made my nest on an air mattress in the concrete sanctum. I washed my clothes, took a shower, and started a book from the shelf, Anne Proulx's *The Shipping News*. I curled up in the living room with the dogs. Zoe the wolf-like dog was still the closest I'd come to seeing a wolf in the flesh, but I hadn't given up hope.

Fish numbers plummeted during this slack time between runs and a seven-to-ten-day closer was announced. It was bad news for skippers, but I took my sentence of a week plus in Cordova with a good spirit. Life at Hawk House was simple and easy. Sometimes Larry or somebody else rallied a crowd to go on an outing on days that weren't completely rained out and miserable. But most days were wet and cold, so I slept an unholy number of hours away and spent much of my waking time with my nose in a book. I read Marcus Zusak's *The Book Thief*, the only book I've read told from Death's perspective. Cormac McCarthy's *The Road* went down in one day. I confess, the lack of structure transformed me into a complete sloth, and I would've been content to read and sleep my life away if it weren't for the gumption of my acquaintances who invited me on adventures.

Larry mustered his offspring—Kara and his fisherman son Zach—and I one grey Cordovan day to go hunting chicken of the woods and king boletus mushrooms. We drove a good way out of town and left the old truck at a deserted trailhead. A cloud of suspicion descended over Larry as we entered the forest, his cheery demeanor forgotten. He glanced up and down the road, an odd exercise as we were clearly alone. Larry saw me stare at him and gestured me close, his gaze dire.

"It doesn't do to give away your mushroom hunting grounds, you know. If the word gets out about this place, it'll be picked barren in a week. Loose lips sink ships, feel me?" Larry growled. I nodded, fearful of what he would do to me if I betrayed him. He patted me on the shoulder and led the way up the trail into an open temperate rain forest. Larry looked like quite the pilgrim with his newsboy cap and walking stick, while Kara, Zach, and I followed, dressed in jeans and hoodies with raincoats as outer shells. The trail wound in and out of forest and bog. Lichen and fungus clung to every inch of wood rot and swamp. We came upon a meadow. Kara pointed to the other side.

"This is where we saw that wolf last year," she said. "He just came out of the woods there and loped on by. A loner."

"Are wolves common around here?" I asked, my voice tinged with excitement. I still had not seen a wolf. Moose and bear, sure. But the wolf, the creature I yearned to see the most, the one I associated with what was pure about the wild and the brother messenger from the spirit world, was still elusive. Kara put her hand to her chin.

"Not really," she said. Larry and Zach fell behind, but I could hear some of their conversation.

"I think I'm going to get my fishing license," Zach said. Larry's eyes wandered for mushrooms, but Zach had his true attention. Obtaining a commercial fishing license was one of the many expensive, necessary steps to becoming a gillnet skipper like Larry. Fishermen who wanted out of the game sold their licenses at whatever price they wanted, usually to the tune of tens of thousands of dollars. The licenses were in strictly limited supply but were good for life to the holder. Alaskan law mandated that only private citizens, not corporations like elsewhere, could hold the licenses.

"Is that so? That sure is a thing," Larry said neutrally. They walked in silence for a time. "Have you any leads? You'll have to get a loan, I imagine." Larry's brow was furrowed, but a small smile played under his mustache. The son was to follow the father, because of, or despite, his wishes.

Noah invited himself into my basement lair in Hawk House one drizzly day and I, half-asleep, rolled over to face my intruder.

"Hey Norris, get up. Let's go to Orca and find a plunger!" Noah stood over me. I blinked and rubbed my eyes.

"Ugh," I muttered. "What time is it?"

"I dunno, like, noon. Let's go. You don't want to pay for one, do you?" Noah asked. The gleam was in his eye, the one from when he wanted to run on the muddy slopes from Shoup Bay to Valdez. I relented, the shame of losing the plunger on my first day now refreshed in mind, and we were out of the house a few minutes later.

Noah walked his bike beside me as he explained that Orca was the name of an abandoned cannery on the outskirts of the town a few miles past the ferry terminal. During the golden days of herring, a whole community was built around Orca. A huge complex known simply as The Bunkhouse housed the hundreds of largely Filipino cannery workers. People even built nice residential homes in the area that developed into a chugging economic engine for the larger Cordova community. But the good old days were over and Cordova was shrinking. The cannery was a cluster of mostly abandoned warehouses, the empty Bunkhouse full of broken windows and graffiti. The cabins were vacant in the forest. There had to be a forgotten plunger somewhere in the decay.

"How far is it?" I asked.

"Two, maybe three miles," Noah said. I nodded and pointed to his bike.

"Get on that thing, I'll run beside ya," I said.

"You sure? Ok," Noah said. He set an easy pace on his bicycle and I jogged at his side. The road took us past the cliffs above the ferry terminal and along the striking coastline of Prince William Sound. We came upon a small boatyard with a handful of old, mostly decrepit boats. Noah paused by a particularly derelict seiner that sat on rusty stands, the faded name *End Zone* on the stern. Grass sprouted on the wooden deck and lichen plastered the hull.

"This is Steve's dad's boat. What a piece of garbage. Hey!" Noah said. He reached onto the deck and lifted an old, but serviceable, plunger.

"Nice," I licked my lips. "Wait, somebody owns this... beauty?" I gestured to the *End Zone*.

"Yeah. But they won't miss this. Let's just take it," Noah reassured me. It was tempting, but I shook my head and sighed. My honor was at stake.

"I've got to ask them first. I can't steal to pay off my debt. I bet they'll give it over or sell it for cheap, right? It's not like they use this stuff," I said. Noah slowly put the plunger back.

"This boat has been like this for years," he mumbled, but we carried on. Rain started to fall, but I ran all the way to Orca, struggling not to mouth breath too hard for dignity's sake. We wandered into the metal and wood warehouse of the dilapidated Orca cannery that sat on large pilings over the tide zone. The cavernous main building was empty save for a forklift in a far corner with the keys still in it. Noah and I nearly took it for a spin, but sadly level heads prevailed. Although Orca was no longer a functioning cannery, some marine related business still went on there. I didn't want to mess up some guy's livelihood. I never was a very good hellraiser.

We exited the cannery and checked the barnacle-encrusted world among the support pilings underneath. Local kids built a budding utopia among the pilings and tide pools. We travelled over a wood plank highway that connected treehouse-like structures made of crudely nailed together two-by-fours. We didn't find anything of use and left. Noah led me into the woods to the infamous Bunkhouse. It leered at us with a smile of broken windows.

"They say one of them hanged himself in one of the rooms and he still haunts the place. Want to check it out?" Noah asked.

"Sure," I said. Cue the creepy music. Noah led me through a door that was clearly pried open by a crowbar. We entered the dim interior of the abandoned warren. The roof had collapsed in places and we picked past mossy drywall and rotten lumber on tiptoes. The doors to all the rooms were missing. Discarded bits of cloth and shards of glass littered the dusty hallway and creaky stairwell. I peeked into a room where a solitary white blouse lay on the floor. Noah kicked a sock in the hallway like a hacky sack. One room was full to brimming with moldy mattresses. Another contained stacks of the missing doors.

We ascended the stairs and came upon a room where the walls were covered in spray paint graffiti. *Die*, *Red Rum*, and *This is where I died* kind of stuff. A lone chair sat in the middle. I paused at the entrance.

"This must be the room, huh?" I asked. A cloud drifted in front of the sun and the already dim scene turned dark.

"Yeah, must be," Noah replied. We poked around for a bit, but I was glad when we left. It would take a lot of guts to spend the night in that horrible place. We left the Orca area after we stopped by one of the cabins in the forest. The one we chose had all its windows intact and looked structurally sound.

"Are you sure these are all abandoned?" I asked as Noah opened the unlocked door with a creak.

"Oh yeah, nobody lives around here anymore," Noah whispered and we entered. The living room was dusty but still furnished. It looked like whoever lived here had just decided to leave on a whim one day. I was reminded of a documentary I saw about Chernobyl and shuddered. A well-used candle on a stand sat on the coffee table.

"Then why are you whispering?" I whispered back.

"I'm not whispering," Noah whispered.

"Yes, you are. We're whispering right now."

"I'm not whispering."

"Yes. You. Are. Whoa," I stopped Noah and pointed to the kitchen. "Why is the light on?" A pitch-black hallway led into the guts of the house to our left.

"Did you hear that?" Noah asked. I heard the creak too.

"Maybe someone is living here. Like a squatter… or a man on the run?" I said. Noah's eyes darted to the shadows.

"Let's go," he suggested. I was already out the door.

I was dispirited on the walk back from Orca. There we were, fresh from a scavenger's paradise and not a single plunger to be found. We passed the yard with the old boats. Two guys our age were aboard the *End Zone*.

"Hey, that's Steve," Noah pointed to one of them and waved. They waved back.

"Really? Let's ask him about the plunger," I suggested. We detoured to the *End Zone*.

"Yo, Noah. How's it going?" Steve jumped off the moss-ridden deck.

"Doing fine, doing fine, yeah," Noah replied. "This is Norris. We're both fishing on the *Solstice*."

"Nice, man. I'm Steve. You guys are doing pretty well, I hear."

"Yeah, can't complain," I replied. We schmoozed for a while before Noah eased the conversation in the direction of the plunger.

"You lost a plunger on day one? That's pretty funny," Steve chuckled.

"Yeah, well, we've been searching Orca all day but couldn't find one," I shook my head. I glanced at the deck of the *End Zone* as if this was the first time I saw it.

"Are you using those plungers?" I asked.

"Can we have one of your plungers? It's not like you'll be going out anytime soon," Noah interjected.

"Yeah, we could really use one," I said. Steve stroked his chin.

"Hmmm... nah, I don't think so," he replied.

"Really? Why not?" I asked. He shook his head.

"Nah, you never know when a plunger is going to come in handy, you know?" Steve said. I gave his boat another once over. The *End Zone* had one foot in the grave.

"Oh c'mon. Really, Steve?" Noah asked. But Steve was a fisherman at heart and already had the penny-pinching mindset.

"Nope," Steve said. We changed the subject. Noah and I split ways once we got into town, he to his family's dinner table and me to the streets of Cordova. I thought I might as well see if Osa had any ideas, so I dropped by the pet store. Her husband was there, a friendly man named Hank who already knew who I was.

"Ah, Norris. Great to see you," Hank shook my hand warmly. I told him of my plunger woes.

"I was going to ask Osa if she had any ideas," I finished.

"Ah, well, she is in Washington D.C.," Hank puffed out his chest.

"Washington, D.C.?" I asked.

"Yes, she just testified against Exxon in the oil spill case. And what a testimony! Quite the lady I've got, beauty *and* brains. Her testimony is going to be archived in the Library of Congress." His eyes were shiny, his pride in his wife a treat to witness.

Hank was right. You can put down this book right now and check out Osa Schultz's testimony online if you want. *HuffPost* was one of the many media outlets that covered Osa's story, calling her "the star witness… and remarkably energetic small-business entrepreneur." They quoted her fundamental question in the article: "If our highest court in America fails to hold [Exxon] accountable, how will they ever be forced to take responsibility for their destructive actions?"

"What a lady indeed. You're a lucky man," I grinned.

"You don't gotta tell me," he said and waved me to his truck. "Get in, I've got an idea." He drove me to a couple marine supply stores, but none of them had plungers for less than the $80 Scott was going to charge me. I thanked the man and ended up at Old Harbor again, reflective in my defeat. The $80 didn't bother me, but I longed to show Scott Brown Jr. my word was good. I wasn't green anymore and to bring him a plunger would've been a redemptive moment to relish.

I walked on the rocks in the tide zone and found a freshly dead seagull. I thought about his life at sea and all he had seen above and below the waves. I wondered if he had dodged a whale's maw while he picked at a bait ball or if he raised any chicks with a mate. He undoubtedly fought, for a seagull's life is full of dogfights. It was a poetic thing, that dead seagull on the rocks, and I wrote about him in my journal.

Back to Work

"What have you been up to, Al?" I asked as he handed me the last crate of iced tea tallboys from Scott Brown Jr.'s truck. An opener was announced after three weeks of closers and at last it was time to fish again. Cordova gave us a classic farewell of overcast skies and drizzling rain. I looked forward to leaving, although I had my fair share of good memories from the long break. There were many jazz-filled nights with the Hawk House Intellectuals and I got drunk for the first time. Beer was growing on me, no longer reminiscent of bitter carbonated bread. As the night wound down and I curled up in bed, I thought I was in the clear, but bolted upright a few hours later to throw up. I fell back asleep and later woke up to Sophie licking my half-digested salmon dinner off the basement floor. I cleaned it up and, so far as I knew, nobody was the wiser. The people who drink the most at parties are certainly the alcoholics, who know the game too well, and the new drinkers, who don't know it at all.

I also got to be Debbie and Larry's designated driver from a beach bonfire. What high school grad wouldn't want the opportunity to D.D. their English teacher? I climbed Mount Eyak with Kara and Zach and saw Child's Glacier with a Hawk House posse. I helped Dora put up meshed supportive material to keep an eroding bank intact for salmon habitat. I nearly went on a multiday marine biology expedition aboard the research vessel *Auklet* but decided against it in case of a surprise fishing opener announcement. I read the unbearable *Are Men Necessary?* by the self-proclaimed too-successful-to-land-a-man, Maureen Dowd.

And I slept. A lot.

Darrell moved back into Hawk House and I was given the polite boot the day before. A lazy, out-of-work deckhand hanging around was a definite mood killer. Time for this stone to keep rolling.

Al shrugged and walked with me to the *Solstice*.

"Screwed around, I dunno. There isn't a skate park around here. I've been bored as balls." We stepped onto the *Solstice*, all set to go. I wrinkled my nose.

"Something smells rank," I waved my hand in front of my face.

"Must be a humpy in the hold," Scott joined us on the deck. "Somebody has got to go in there and get it." He looked at us one at a time. I sighed and reached for my work gloves. The white curtain of seagulls near the cannery parted for our passage.

"I'm on it," I said.

I removed a hatch board and lowered myself into the dank hold. We cast off and were just leaving the harbor when I located the rancid salmon body in the darkest corner. I emerged with a victorious smile and held the limp, rotten fish up to Noah's face.

"Dinner, anybody?" I asked. Noah backed up.

"That's nasty. Chuck it!"

"With pleasure," I declared and threw the foul thing into the sea. Ten gulls dove upon it and squabbled for a bite. One nickel less for me. I put my smelly gloves in the locker and joined the rest of the crew in the cabin.

"It's my game. Gimme!" Anthony whined to Al, who held the Wii guitar over his head out of Anthony's reach.

"You just played, like, four songs. It's my turn!" Al yelled. Noah looked to me and rolled his eyes. I beamed. The band was back together again. I slid past the squabble and climbed the ladder to the wheelhouse as *Free Bird* started to play on the TV.

"Permission to join, skip," I asked Scott who watched the wheel.

"Sure," Scott said. I joined him and we gazed out at the view. We were hardly ten minutes out of Cordova and already the clouds began to clear. The *Solstice* cruised over the gentle creases of the sound, the water colored gold by the setting sun just like our first departure months ago. We were an iron steaming over the wrinkles of an endless yellow dress. Scott pointed to an exposed stretch of rock on a point.

"Back when I was student body prez, some of the high school girls in town spray-painted 'We Love You Scott' on that rock," Scott said. He looked over his shoulder at me, an uncharacteristically toothy grin across his face. "Those were some good times."

"I was student body president too, but girls didn't paint anything for me on a rock," I laughed. Scott gave a curt nod as if to say, 'you bet they didn't' and tended to our course.

The *Solstice* was a painted stroke of a landscape masterpiece the next day. We anchored a stone's throw from shore somewhere near Unakwik, a good position for next day's opener. Noah brought an inflatable raft for this run. Anthony's new kayak rested on deck. A fishing pole made an appearance. All of uninhabited Alaska stretched before us. We decided to go ashore.

Our armada stormed the beach, us crew in the raft and Anthony in his kayak. A tidepool the size of a football field was cradled in the forest and a trapped school of salmon—probably a good two thousand pounds—swam in lazy circles. Al jumped into Anthony's kayak and snatched his pole.

"That's mine, nigga," Anthony said.

"I'll give it back, just gimme a minute," Al snapped and launched Anthony's kayak into the tidepool. He cast the hook into the middle of the salmon and reeled in. "I snagged one! Ha!"

Sure enough, a fish struggled against the hook in her side. Al pulled his prize aboard and threw it back.

"Cool," said Noah. He rowed his raft onto the pond. "Let me try."

"Hey. That's mine!" Anthony whined from shore. I put my hand on his shoulder.

"We'll get our chance. Want to explore?" I gestured to the untouched forest around us and the rolling green hills above. Anthony glowered at the kayak.

"I guess," he muttered. We marched off into the brush. I gasped.

"Anthony, these are all—"

"Blueberries!" Anthony cheered. We started picking. The blueberries were like grapes on the bushes. I devoured a hundred of them without taking a step. We gorged before we resumed our trek up a hill, our lips stained blue.

"Bear," I said and pointed to a pile of dung rich with blueberry seeds.

"Dayum right, nigga!" Anthony skipped ahead.

"Stop saying that!" I yelled and chased after him. The sun pierced the clouds with beams of heavenly light. We ran right under one. No angles sang for us, so we did it ourselves. Mountains loomed ahead, likely famous number Bazillion and number Bazillion-and-one. I asked Anthony to take a picture. I struck a pose, my chest out and my hands on my hips. Anthony wanted a picture too, and he posed in the same way with a smug smirk on his face. A worthy parody.

Inlets twisted around islands and fjords while seiners speckled the bay below. I could see some familiar hulls like the *Mantis* and the *Heathen*. I didn't see the *Praetorian* and reckoned Scott would miss Maggie's presence. I stayed up there for a while after Anthony went down to the tidepool to try the pole. I gazed out over the water and saw five jumpers in less than a minute.

Unakwik is paradise.

I walked down the hill to the others. Anthony cast his pole from Noah's raft. There were so many damned salmon trapped in the pond that somebody could build a rock barrier to keep them there at high tide and live forever. Salmon so thick you just had to cast a hook and reel 'em in. They didn't even need to bite.

"Gimme the pole, Anthony," Al tried to yank the pole from Anthony's hands.

"No, it's mine!" Anthony tried to keep it away.

"You little shit, gimme it," Al huffed. I lay on the beach and smiled at them bickering. Unakwik was paradise. We stayed out there all day, catching salmon, walking around, eating berries. Anthony picked up smooth flat rocks and wrote our names on them with blueberry juice. He gave me mine shyly when we arrived back on the *Solstice*.

"Anthony, this is awesome, thank you," I said. I kept it on the little shelf above my berth like a talisman for the rest of the season. I'm not sure if the other guys cared as much about their rocks, but damn it, I loved mine. I wished bitterly that Anthony's leather-bound journal had arrived during the long closer in Cordova. His birthday present was long overdue.

"Soon Anthony, I swear. A present from Italy." I promised.

"You're lying," Anthony pointed at me. "Liar liar, pants on fire!"

"You'll see," I gritted my teeth. After we returned to the *Solstice*, somebody put on the movie *Fight Club*. Al whispered things like 'that's so badass' under his breath. Noah and I played chess. He was a more practiced player than I was, but I beat him the first two times we played. I figured out he was skittish to sacrifice and it was easy to control the battlefield. I was all for the sacrifice and as long as I controlled the terms of the sacrifices, I always came out slightly ahead. When it came down to a handful of pieces left, I kept up the attack and won. It was easier for me to lead a small group of troops than a hulking army. Simplify, simplify. I don't think Noah liked my style and stopped playing with me, but he'd have whooped me if I didn't play reckless.

Noah cooked up a halibut steak dinner, much to Scott's delight. The skipper always liked it when one of us stepped up to cook. Anthony showed off his newly constructed Lego seiner, an incredible piece of creativity. It had the winches in the right places, a wheelhouse, the hydraulic boom, and a hold in the deck. It wasn't even a bought set. Anthony let Al borrow the expensive airsoft gun James had given him. The word was that James quit the *Rikki-Tikki-T* midway through the season and blew what money he did earn on a gas-guzzling, beat-up truck.

"That kid is a moron," Scott Brown Jr., James' idol, said simply. I knew what really bothered Scott about James' move. James was now permanently demoted to quitter status, something I didn't think Scott could ever bring himself to forgive. I went to bed happy that I wasn't one. I was a fisherman on a highliner and we were going to catch some salmon tomorrow.

0500 hours, awake.

0600 hours, ready.

The band was back together, baby.

Highliners coming through.

High. Liners.

Unakwik was a more open field of play than the Valdez run was, but this was both a blessing and a curse. Scott Brown Jr. didn't have a magic spot like Shoup Bay to camp out near, and the *Solstice* hopped around and set with just a handful of boats in any given lineup. The biggest sets we pulled in were around 5,000 pounds, nothing to write home about but nothing to scoff at either. The big difference for me was that we weren't waiting in long lineups.

The work to rest ratio was thus skewed, but I figured I could keep this up until the closer. Whenever that was.

One day, the messenger line—a support line that attaches the seine to the boat through the power block—unclipped itself while the seine soaked. I said as much and grabbed the line and shackle from where it swung from the power block on my march to the stern. I would have to crawl over the taunt deployed seine to the clip to reattach the line, a short tightrope crawl over the ocean.

"Careful," Scott warned.

"I got this," I assured and put the messenger line shackle in my teeth. I sank onto my hands and knees to shuffle over the taunt seine. The whitewash from the prop gurgled and growled beneath me, churning up the green water. Miracle water. I clipped it in and was back on deck in no time. Scott nodded once.

"Nice job, Point Dexter," he said. I basked in the sunlight of his praise the whole day.

Another set was a real pain in the ass. The seine just wouldn't come in. Scott, Al, and I wrestled with the giant tea bag containing a few thousand pounds of fish for an hour before—*Kaboom!*—something blew from below.

Scott Brown Jr. radioed Scott Brown Sr., who dropped by for a look at the busted generator. While the two skippers were below, Amy Brown—Senior's wife, Junior's mom, and Anthony's grandma—came aboard with a piping-hot cauldron of homemade chili. She wore a pair of horned thick-rimmed glasses. Her dyed blonde, aggressively ironed hair and bright pink lipstick made it hard for me to judge her age.

"Thanks, Mrs. Brown," we cheered. Amy beamed.

"I wouldn't want you hard working boys going hungry," Amy cooed.

"Fuck! Cunt fuckin' dicksucker!" Senior roared from below. Amy didn't bat an eyelash.

"It's the *Time Bandit*. It's the *Time Bandit*, guys!" Anthony pointed across the sound. The *Solstice* crew lounged on the seine while Scott Brown Jr. motored around, still hungry for a money spot. I turned to see a large black tender. Sure enough, she was the iconic *Time Bandit* with the skull and crossbones on the bow from Discovery Channel's wildly popular commercial crabbing reality TV show *Deadliest Catch*. I, like so many other suburbanites in the lower forty-eight who felt insulated from adventure, loved *Deadliest Catch*.

"No way," I said. I jumped to my feet to get a better look. "That's awesome." I squinted into the sun. "That's the Hillstrand brothers, right?"

"Wow-wee!" Anthony crowed and we jumped up and down. I jogged into the cabin and returned with my binoculars.

"Jesus Christ," Al cut in. "You guys are embarrassing."

"But it's the *Time Bandit*," I withered under his gaze. Scott looked down at Anthony and me with amused disappointment from the wheelhouse.

"Yeah, what's so special about those guys?" Noah asked.

Al nodded in agreement.

"They are just fuckin' lucky is all," Al said. I calmed down, but swept the deck with my binoculars. It was true, the crew and skippers of the show seemed so solitary and larger-than-life when taking on the Bering Sea on TV. In reality, they were no more respectable nor badass than the many other crabbers of the fleet or the thousands of other fishermen in Alaska. I'd even heard that the crabbers off Oregon had more casualties and injuries per capita. Later in life, I learned even more bubble-popping news. The crabbing boats turn on cue to take the seas abeam to get their dramatic shots for the cameras. Crabbers don't even fish when the weather sours too bad, also not something talked about on the show.

The more I thought about it, the sillier I felt. Hell, in another universe where the cameras pointed in another direction, the salmon seiners might've been the badasses and Scott Brown Jr. a national celebrity.

I spied two sets of neon pink bikinis and long tanned legs on the deck.

"Well, maybe you're right, but they've got a few babes on board," I said.

"Let me see," Al jumped up and I handed him the binoculars. The sight of the hotties on the *Time Bandit* twisted his expression into an envious grimace. "Fuckin' lucky, man."

The wind-down at night was an essential part of those grinder days. We shed our fish-smelling raingear in the locker and shambled into the cabin. If we were lucky enough to beat the offloading rush and deliver our catch first, we could be in our berths as early as nine or ten o'clock. However, being the first to offload was hardly the norm. Typically, we were done around midnight. Sometimes one or two in the morning.

Scott always vanished into the wheelhouse after work was done. We wouldn't see him again until morning. Noah, Al, and I sat around the table or piled into the v-berth. We usually started by talking about fishing. There was some high point to rehash, like a notable set or our paycheck for the day. There was also a low point, like a purse line fuck up or our paycheck for the day. There was always something different to laugh about or a horror story from another boat in the fleet to share.

A deckhand on another boat was caught by outgoing gear and dragged into the sea. A nearby skiffman from a different boat saved the kid's life with quick thinking, brawn, and knife. The word was that the skipper of the boat with the nearly drowned kid always had his deckhands work in the danger zone at the stern as the seine went out. When his half-drowned deckhand was returned to him, the skipper put him right back to work in the danger zone. The skipper was officially an asshole.

121

Another crew lost their seine to a whale. The giant filter feeder swam right into the net as it soaked. They might as well have caught a nuclear submarine. The crew unclipped their gear and never saw it again.

Anthony would sometimes goof off with us before going to bed with his dad. I remember having trouble sleeping one night and listened to the faint voices of the two in the wheelhouse.

"Nyah nyah nyah," Anthony goaded his father. Scott's laughter was tired and rumbling.

"You little fucker," he muttered lovingly. I pictured the two of them up there under the glow of a cabin light, surrounded by the blackness of night that peered in through the windows of the wheelhouse. When I read Cormac McCarthy's post-apocalyptic *The Road* in Hawk House, I thought of Scott Brown Jr. as the man and Anthony as the boy. Father and son against the world.

I was a machine during the day. An increasingly overworked, black smoke spewing machine. Unakwik, with its never-ending opener and wide-open space, was a free for all. Often there were just one or two boats in a line, which translated to nearly constant sets. The Valdez schedule of working for a day or two with an hour or more between sets and then getting a day or two off was a pleasant dream. A three-day opener led to an announcement of a four-day opener. I stopped hoping for a closer break. It was too hard to hope.

Despite working five times as hard, we were usually producing about 16,000 pounds a day. Sometimes twenty-something. 37,000 pounds was our max. We had to grind out our paycheck now, squeeze every day for what it was worth. Things started to get screwy. One day we somehow tore a big hole in the seine. We had to back haul and Scott Brown Jr. patched it up with his threader. Our purse line snapped another day and luckily Scott Brown Sr. had a spare. We had to back-haul the seine again to thread the new purse line.

Poor Noah began to feel the brunt of the pressure. Scott moved spots daily and Noah had to adapt quickly. Scott got upset at Noah for one set where Noah didn't hug the beach closely enough. Apparently, we missed most of the school and the seiner behind us scooped them up, no problem. Like I said before, as a sweaty deckhand, I wanted to be the skiffman ninety percent of the time. But for that ten percent of the time, I wouldn't do it for the world.

Those grinder days were killing me and it got harder to crack a smile. As the run dragged on, Al remained in good spirits. He'd usually be sucking away at a Fireball candy. One day I even caught him whistling while he plunged.

"Dude, how are you so happy?" I asked. Al's brows rose. "I mean it. You've always got this dopey smile on your face and you're just chugging along like a champ. How do you do it? I'm a friggin' zombie." A sheepish grin spread across Al's face. He leaned in real close.

"I'm high as balls, man," Al whispered.

"What?" I laughed. Everything became clear. That explained the Fireball candy and the great attitude.

"Exactly, dude. The candy hides the smell," Al said. He took off his purple beanie and sniffed it. "Mostly."

Scott emerged and gave Noah the order to close up. Al kept plunging while I readied the towline for the toss into the skiff. Scott's face was bright red. He leaned heavily against the rail overlooking the deck. It dawned on me that Anthony and I could be the only two sober ones aboard.

Huh.

I looked at Noah approaching in the skiff. I wondered what Noah was on. Cocaine? Adderall? Noah completed a hurried seine hand off and hustled alongside to receive the towline. Scott had been riding him about doing it all faster. Al and I talked with Noah earlier about how we could help. We just weren't sure how. Noah didn't have any ideas. Scott just wanted it faster somehow.

Noah bumped his skiff into the side of the *Solstice*. I pelted the towline. *Clunk!* I had yet to miss a throw. Noah clipped in and tore off at full towing speed, eager to get the pressure off him for the set. However, the towline was wrapped around the skiff's center console. In Noah's haste, he had forgotten to fairlead it.

Var-ROOOM! The engine of the skiff groaned as the towline took tension at high throttle. The skiff pitched to the side against the taut line wrapped around the console like a mad dog against a leash. Noah was tossed overboard.

"Hey!" I yelled. Noah somehow twisted his body midair as the runaway skiff flew over the water. He clung onto the skiff like a rodeo cowboy to the side of a runaway bronco. His feet flailed for a purchase on the smooth aluminum hull.

"Holy shit!" Al yelled.

"Noah, get back in there!" Scott roared, helpless.

"Fuck!" I joined the chorus. Noah's body visibly trembled with the Herculean effort of holding on. The skiff reached the end of its leash and twisted again with a splash. Noah banged against the side of the skiff's hull and his entire lower body disappeared into the water. His grip on the gunnel was all that kept him from falling into the drink. We cussed from the deck as the rogue boat changed course toward the stern of the *Solstice*.

The skiff was going to hit us. If Noah ended up between the two boats, he was a goner.

KH-unk! Scott and I leapt aboard the crashed skiff as it rammed us. Scott turned down the throttle. I reached over the side and wrapped Noah up under the armpits to hoist him aboard with adrenaline and deckhand brawn. Noah, miraculously, was not a gory pancake.

Scott brought him into the cabin to dry. Al and I high fived and tried to calm down.

"Holy shit dude, did you see that?" Al crowed.

"That was insane!" I howled. We rode a crazy high, man. I couldn't even imagine what that must've been like for Al while stoned. Noah returned to the deck for work after a short break. We tried to pump him up, but he was down on himself. I'm telling ya, for that ten percent of the time, I'd rather not fish at all than be the skiffman.

Those grinders were rough. Scott Brown Jr. was always on the move; quiet, stressed, and buzzed. He had yet to find our spot, the place that would pay off. The new Shoup. The only part of the day that offered relief was when the crew was so slap happy with exhaustion before bed that we'd stay up and talk. We shined a lamp on the ceiling to make shadow puppet animals when Anthony sneaked down to join us in the v-berth. Al's long fingers made the best spider. Anthony's tiny butterfly usually lost shape when he flapped it too quickly. Noah mastered the nuanced finger placement for the most convincing dog. We laughed in quiet voices and a stream of tired, warm rumbling flowed from our glowing den. Those shadow puppet shows kept me going.

The Great Net

"**U**nakwik isn't a paradise. In fact, it might be a hell," states my journal, August 15, 2008. The day of wild blueberries and sunshine must've been a dream. The real Unakwik was cold and rainy. The real Unakwik had more jellies than humpies. The real Unakwik tore our seine open, busted our lines, and worked us to the bone for every measly pound. The real Unakwik was going to kill us.

One day was so awful that Scott Brown Jr. declared we were going to deliver our few hundred pounds early and make a run for a place called Esther, "Before I shoot myself." We, the crew, peeled off our rubber skins after the meager delivery as Scott pushed the *Solstice*'s maximum cruising speed to Esther. Noah looked to me and made a brushing gesture with his hand across his chin.

"You've got a bit of, ah—" Noah started. I reached to my chin and flicked off a stray gob of jellyfish. My whole face stung. The rest of me was too numb from the cold and exercise to feel. We pillaged the bags of chips, boxes of pop tarts, and sandwich fixings before settling around the table. Anthony asked if I could boil some water for him to make rice and he kept busy in the galley.

"This fucking sucks," Al groaned. "We're not catching balls, man." I noticed that he wasn't sucking on a Fireball candy anymore.

"Are you out?" I asked.

He nodded gravely. Welcome to sober hell, man.

Al leaned across the table. His voice lowered.

"Last night, I saw Scott drinking Listerine. Like, chugging it," Al said.

"Wow, are you sure? That's crazy," Noah said.

"I swear, man," Al said. His brow furrowed.

"Like, Listerine mouthwash? Why would he do that?" I asked.

"It's got alcohol in it," Noah answered. Al nodded.

"Fuckin' alcoholics drink that shit," Al said.

"Hey, we don't know," I started. "I guess that means he's out of boxed wine. Dry as a bone now. Just like the rest of us."

"Norris, *ugh*!" Anthony's voice cut me off from the kitchen.

"What?" I asked.

"You didn't add enough water. My rice is all burnt cause of you, you dummy," Anthony sneered.

"I put in what you asked me, Anthony. You must've added too much rice or something," I said.

"No, you messed up the rice. What the hell, nigga?" Anthony came to the table and leered in my face. He waved a wooden spoon with burnt rice on it for emphasis.

"Stop saying that word, Anthony! And I didn't have anything to do with your rice, I just put water to boil like you asked me to—" I began.

"Yeah, shut the fuck up you little shit!" Al exploded. "For fuck's sake, you're driving us insane. We fucking hate you!" Anthony clenched his jaw, his eyes shiny, and ran to the galley. There was a terrific clatter of pots before he stormed past us and up to the wheelhouse. I groaned and put my head in my hands.

Surely, the day of sunshine and wild blueberries was a dream.

The real Unakwik was going to kill us.

The Esther lineup was so long that we only got one set for the whole day. It was a break my body appreciated but drove Scott to the brink. Scott, sober and restless for a change of fortune, left to gamble at another place called Kaniklik. We would've been first in line at Esther the next day and for the first time I began to doubt Scott's judgment. Why not at least scoop up the first set before leaving tomorrow? We entered the cabin from the one Esther set in downtrodden spirits. A platter of hot fudgy brownies sat on the table.

"Hell yeah," Al said. He and I shoved brownies down our gullets in fistfuls of delicious warm goo.

"Where did these come from?" Noah asked, the only one of us who ate the brownies one at a time like a civilized person.

"Anthony made them," Scott said as he walked past on his way to the wheelhouse. "He thought you guys were mad at him." I glanced to Al, who slowed his chewing and gazed off at nothing. "You know, he told me the other day that you were his favorite crew. Just thought you ought to know. He's been around a lot of them." Scott left that thought in the air before he vanished up the ladder. We polished off the plate in silence before he rejoined us.

"Hey, where's mine?" Scott asked. We scattered.

Kaniklik wasn't any better. We wandered around the greater Unakwik area, shooting from the hip and following radio gossip. Bad juju abounded. The purse line managed to come completely out of the seine once. Another set was a real devil to get in. Who knew why?

"Cocksucker!" Scott howled. He blasted the power block at full speed. It took everything I had to keep up, but I did. Al and I were too tired afterward to brag about it to each other.

Scott did deliver a piece of good news that slowed the downward spiral of morale. The price of pink salmon leapt from twenty-seven cents per pound to thirty-five. Noah's eyes popped out of his head as I scribbled new calculations in my journal.

"You're shitting me," Al exclaimed.

"Nope," Scott said. "What this means is that after another 19,400 pounds, you'll all have $20,000 crew shares." Scott left us in high spirits, a rare sight these days. I had grown so accustomed to his wheelhouse brooding that I'd forgotten how good it felt when the skipper was happy.

"Twenty G's, bro," Al sat back with his hands behind his head. Anthony joined us and we wrestled with him playfully before crowding into the v-berth for shadow puppets and bedtime chatter. I was just about to close my eyes when I realized I had to take a piss. I sighed and rolled out of the v-berth and onto the deck in my boxers.

The void of space was saturated with an impossible number of stars. I yawned and started to urinate off the side, one hand driving and the other scratching my side. The sea was as still as a pool. The stars and red moon reflected so perfectly I couldn't tell where Earth and the cosmos met. I was pissing off a spaceship. The water I disturbed frothed with tiny, brilliant green lights. Bioluminescence. I tried to write my name but ran out of juice.

"They'll find my bones in Unakwik," states my journal. The morning was absolute misery. I managed to slide into my rubber skins, more of a habit than anything. I closed my eyes in the cabin and slumped over where I listened for the "Get ready!" command and dreamed of my bed. And Genevieve. Sometimes I wonder if I'm still mourning that loss.

"Eyes open," Scott's voice intruded my peace. I forced them open. The world was blurry. "No sleeping. Time for work."

"Yes, Scott," I murmured. His icy blue floodlights bore into me for a few seconds before he disappeared into the wheelhouse. I stumbled onto the deck like I was freshly mugged, another grinder in Unakwik awaiting me. We were in a small inlet with only the *Mantis* and a random seiner from California for company. This was the day Anthony was to go home. School started soon. Scott Brown Sr. on the *Mantis* was cashing in his chips for the season, for the run hadn't been much easier for him. Anthony was to hitch a ride with gramps back to Cordova. Even Noah and Al doubted they would fish out the humpy season or the upcoming silver run, the one-day, derby-style season in early September.

Anthony emerged from the cabin, a baseball cap on his head and a duffle bag of his stuff over his shoulder.

"Bye, Anthony," I smiled as he made the jump onto the *Mantis*.

"Peace out, nigga!" Anthony said. He disappeared into the cabin of the *Mantis* as it motored away. The mood grew heavier in Anthony's absence even though I knew Al would never admit it. The little gremlin had kept us on our toes with his antics, a trail of laughter and curses in his wake. Without him we were a bunch of overworked stiffs.

I looked to the seiner from California. We were going to take turns working the spot all day, at once both a duel and a dance. The only limits were the speed of the crews and the reliability of the machinery. No breaks today. Noah was ready in the skiff, the poor guy jittery after weeks of extra pressure on him and now a new spot to learn. Al was ready on the deck, one cool cat.

"Go!" Scott yelled.

Bear trap released.

Seine soaking.

Time to plunge.

"I don't think this life is for me," I broke the popping rhythm of plunging.

"What do you mean?" Al asked over a plunger thrust. *Pop!*

"This life, man. Sucking all the fish out of the sea for money and all the stress around the money. I don't know. It's just money, money, money—"

Pop! "I thought I'd escape the money thing up here, you know? Joke's on me." *Pop!*

"Well, if you don't like it, you probably shouldn't do it," Al suggested. *Pop!*

"I'm finishing out this season unlike you, schoolboy," I teased. Al scowled.

"See, I'd rather be out here all year. I hate school, it's a bunch of bullshit. I think I'd like to fish on my dad's boat next season though." *Pop!* "I mean, what the fuck? I'm making more money than my teachers out here and I'm doing something much more useful than fucking being in a classroom somewhere. Feel me? I don't need their bullshit, why the fuck do I need to know shit about chemistry?"

I took a minute to study Al as he plunged. He liked his weed, chicks, skateboards, and doing crazy shit. He was a fisherman like his ancestors before him. I doubt I'll ever meet a man more content with his lot in life than Allen Bishop was in that moment. I sort of fell in love with him, kind of like how I understood Scott Brown Jr. that one night during the Valdez run over deer tortellini. Al made sense in an honest, open way. How could I not love how genuine he was?

Noah was closing up the seine, so we got into our positions. I prayed to the powers of the universe that this was our last day. Blow out the engine. Have a whale take the net. The *Mantis* was going home with Anthony, and if that wasn't an omen, I didn't know what was. I didn't care about a $20,000 crew share. We already had more money than I ever could've imagined when scheming before high school graduation.

I handed Noah the towline. Scott fed the purse line to the deck winch. I went to the stern with a plunger to make sure the net's webbing didn't get tangled with the prop. At least it wasn't raining.

I thought about what to do after the season was over. I made a $100 bet with a friend in high school that I'd try to climb Mt. Denali and going to Denali National Park was a natural first step. I began to daydream of a post-season camping trip. Perhaps I'd finally see a wolf.

The deck winch made a strange crunching noise behind me.

"Ah! Ah! *Ah!*" Scott Brown Jr.'s voice half screamed, half yelped.

Odd. I never heard Scott, or anybody, sound like that before.

"Holy shit! *Holy shit!*" Al's voice was hoarse with panic. I turned about. Scott's whole body spun in the deck winch, limp as a scarecrow in a drying machine. Al jumped up and down at Scott's side, yelling holy shit at the top his lungs and flailing to get Scott free. But Scott spun, his body making wet crunching sounds as he went. I saw his face pass above the deck winch, his teeth gritted and blue eyes darting as he struggled against the wraps of line that bound him to the machine. His boots appeared the next second, pointed up to the sky as he went around and around and around.

I ran to the hydraulic switches, the ones I generally avoided because Scott worked them. I flipped the correct switch and the deck winch froze. Al and I stared at Scott in the new silence for a second trapped in molasses. His right arm was pinned under coils of line and barely attached to his body. He was completely trounced, his face bloodied from a broken nose. His ice-blue eyes roamed back and forth, somehow calm and frantic at the same time. He was stuck half-standing in the winch, his body impossibly twisted. His labored breaths sounded like broken ribs.

"I need...medical... assistance," Scott wheezed.

Time unstuck.

Al and I raced to our cell phones in the cabin.

"I don't have reception here," Al cried. I cursed us bitterly.

"We're idiots, the radio!" I spat. Scott yelled something and Al ran out to him while I climbed the ladder into the wheelhouse. Coast Guard was channel 16. One of the VHFs on board was always tuned to the channel. I clutched the receiver. I didn't know what to say, so I fell back to what I saw on the movie *A Perfect Storm* and accidentally hailed a proper mayday. It went something like this.

"Mayday, mayday, mayday, this is the fishing vessel *Solstice*. Our skipper has been sucked into the deck winch. He… he is doing really bad. We need medical assistance." I let go of the speaker button and clenched the receiver tight enough to break it.

"Fishing vessel *Solstice*, this is Coast Guard—"

A response!

The skiff from the Californian seiner, who like all fishing vessels monitored Channel 16, motored over while I talked to the Coast Guard. I gave the coasties our coordinates, description of our vessel, and some other information they asked for before Noah appeared in the cabin. I gave him the radio. He had more experience with it than I did as a skiffman.

I went out to the deck where Al had backed up the winch so Scott could lay down, a gruesome but necessary task that may have further broken a few bones. Scott's arm was still pinned to the winch by coils of line. Was removing him a good idea? For all we knew, the pressure of the line on his wound was the only thing keeping him from bleeding out.

I greeted the men who arrived from the skiff. One of them, a young, fit-looking fellow, said the most beautiful words I ever could've hoped to hear.

"My name is Eric and I'm an EMT. I'm here to help until the Coast Guard arrives. What seems to be the matter?" I took the EMT and a handful of other good Samaritans to the deck winch and we huddled around Scott. The first step was to ascertain whether or not removing him from the deck winch would kill him. The EMT conferred with the Coast Guard. More skiffs with additional good Samaritans from gathering seiners joined. I don't remember how many.

"He is still in the deck winch?!" The operator was aghast over the VHF. "Get him out!" The men drew their knives and cut Scott free. The EMT led the effort to lift Scott clear and eased him onto the working deck. He turned to me after strapping a supplemental oxygen mask to Scott's face.

"We need to do what we can to mitigate him going into shock. Can you find something that we can prop his feet on? Also, we need blankets to keep him warm."

"On it," I said and made a beeline for the cabin. I found a large Cheerio box to prop up Scott's feet and grabbed Anthony's stray Spiderman blanket. A skipper from a third boat kept pressure on the arm wound. The EMT readied a tourniquet and quick clot. Scott Brown Jr. was pale, his skin clammy. He was going into shock. The Coast Guard was nowhere in sight.

"How's it look?" Scott croaked, his good arm draped over his eyes.

"It's going to be ok, Scott," the EMT said. "Help is on the way."

"Fuck," Scott groaned, seeing through the bullshit.

"Scott," I said and knelt next to him on the deck. His good hand found mine.

He clenched my hand, palm-to-palm.

His grip was still strong.

I squeezed back.

"You are a tough motherfucker, do you hear me? You're the toughest guy I've ever met." I licked my lips and half yelled, half begged. "You have to live, think of your son! Don't you go dying on him, you got that? Don't you dare! The chopper is going to be here any minute. You're going on that fucking thing to the hospital—"

"The father is almost back," one of the guys on a radio told the group of good Samaritans on deck with us. "Senior."

"Don't let my son see!" Scott howled. "Don't let him see me like this!"

"We won't let him see any of this, you have my word," I said. I turned to the man with the radio. "His eleven-year-old son is aboard that boat. He was with us the whole season but got on a few hours ago to get a ride with his grandpa back to Cordova to start school."

"Christ," somebody whispered. The skipper keeping the pressure on the wounded man's nearly amputated arm shook his head.

"Why don't I quit?" Scott groaned. His skin was pale as death and his head shook from side to side like it had a will of its own. He let go of my hand and rested it over his face.

"Why don't I just fuckin' quit?" the dying fisherman asked the universe.

"Nobody is quittin' nothin'," another skipper said.

The *Mantis* arrived and came alongside. Senior and Amy joined the crowd on the deck of the *Solstice* to help. They did not shed a tear like the movies. Action is what their son needed now. Senior didn't stay long and recruited Noah and Al to load the *Solstice*'s gear. Our seine was still deployed and a potential rescue obstacle.

The Coast Guard reassured us that the helicopter was on its way. We ended up lying to Scott about an imminent ETA for one, maybe even two, hours before we heard the thudding of chopper blades. The helicopter lowered a swimmer with a cable to assess the scene. The swimmer wore enough exotic gear to belong to an advanced alien race.

"Whoever isn't part of the loading team, get inside," the swimmer ordered. He packaged Scott onto a backboard and helicopter cradle. Most of the good Samaritans and I ran into the cabin and closed the door as the helicopter descended for the pick-up. Amy crouched over her son, her hair a blonde whirlwind. Scott's pale, unconscious face behind the oxygen mask was about all I could see of him in the cradle. The wind from the chopper depressed the sea, a divine palm pressing from the heavens. We crowded around the porthole of the cabin and watched as Scott and the swimmer were lifted into the sky. The chopper was away. All that remained was a bloody deck and a gathering of fisherfolk.

I shook the hands of everybody I could and thanked them before I fell into line under Senior's direction. Anthony came aboard very briefly, probably to grab something he forgot when he left earlier.

"Was dad hurt?" Anthony asked. I turned around. He held up his Spiderman blanket. It was covered in Scott's blood.

"Yes, baby," Amy said and plucked the blanket out of Anthony's hands.

"Well, that's dumb," Anthony huffed and the two of them boarded the *Mantis*. Senior left his skiffman Lance to act as interim skipper and we solemnly delivered our haul for the day. Al was on hydraulics and did a fine job. Noah and I went into the hold with our short shovels until every salmon was out of there. I don't remember the words exchanged. I looked at the numbers as Lance steamed a course for Cordova on the heels of the *Mantis*. We made our $20,000 crew shares.

Defiance

I awoke alone in Cordova aboard the *Solstice* and spent an hour on my back gazing at the ceiling of the v-berth. Al was probably reunited with his family. Maybe his dad was done fishing and back in town. Noah must've been with his parents and little brother. Both were probably getting ready for school. Anthony too, wherever he was. I bet his grandparents, Senior and Amy, were looking after him.

I heard the thudding of chopper blades.

I rolled out of bed.

There was no helicopter in the sky.

I entered the head and looked in the mirror, something I couldn't get away with for long when others were aboard. I took off my shirt. I was built like a gorilla. A life of labor and a diet heavy in salmon, halibut, venison, and moose burger had really packed on the muscle. My chest was a solid oak barrel, my arms thick and brawny. My hair was long, down to my shoulders long, and curled at the ends with a few silver specks of salmon scales. I had scruff befitting a feral boy, more than stubble but less than a true beard. My blue eyes were dull, listless.

I made bull's eyes for breakfast to distract myself. The hiss of them cooking was comforting even if I wasn't hungry. A few of them were forced down. The sudden urgent need to shower struck, so I gathered my toiletry

137

kit and mealy clothes into my red duffle and slung it over my shoulder. I stumbled onto the streets of Cordova like I was drunk or something, Hawk House my goal. A truck pulled up next to me. My eyes drifted to the driver. It was James.

"Hey, bro," James said. The rumors were true, he had quit his job on the *Rikki-Tikki-T* and blown his cash on a great clunker of an old truck. His ride had more in common with a WWI tank than a pickup. Hunter was in the passenger seat. Neither of them smiled, perhaps it was because of my melancholy air. Maybe they were upset with me. Or genuinely distraught at Scott's misfortune. I didn't care.

"Hey, James," I said, tired.

"Heard about all that shit with Scott," James said. "He is all right though, right?" He searched my eyes, hungry for information. "He's alive, right?"

"I don't know the latest, but he was mangled up pretty bad," I trailed off. "Last I heard he coded twice en route to Anchorage on the chopper." I didn't want to talk to the quitter who, in a not so different world, would've worked on the *Solstice* instead of me. Would've seen what I had seen.

"Yeah, well, Scott will bounce back. He's a beast. If you see him, tell him I want to fish for him next season. Do me a solid?" James asked.

"Sure," I managed. "But he doesn't like that you quit the *Rikki-Tikki-T*." James glared at me.

"Cool, see ya bro," James peeled away in a black cloud of toxic fumes. I coughed and continued on my way with my red duffel bag. All I wanted to do was get in a hot shower and leave it running forever. I was filthy and lonely, mortality a heavy yoke to bear.

I walked down the main drag to say hello to Dora at her office. It wouldn't do to surprise her and Darrell unannounced. Dora leapt from her chair behind her desk and wrapped me in a hug, despite the fact that I smelled like a dead thing at low tide. She was dressed in her power clothes, her spotless headquarters all white walls and shiny wood varnish. I felt even more like a feral caveman. Scott Brown Jr.'s injury was the talk of the town.

"There is talk about 'the deckhand' who saved Scott's life. Is that you?" Dora asked. I cringed.

"I helped, but I don't really deserve that," I said.

"Well, there is already a plan in the works for a big benefit dinner for Scott to raise money for his medical bill, provided he pulls through. He is uninsured," Dora said. I gritted my teeth.

"Damned cowboy," I muttered. We were in the middle of a productive office space and the handful of workers watched us from behind their computer screens. Live theater. I nodded to my duffel bag. "Can I still do laundry and take a shower up in Hawk House?"

"Of course. I'm glad you stopped by," Dora said. It felt good to smile and I stumbled back onto the streets with a little more vitality. I was about to make a beeline for Hawk House, but I was still numb, dead to the world. I needed company to come alive. Osa was the sort of insightful confidant who I craved so I made a detour to the pet store. Perhaps she had inspiring stories from her stand in Washington D.C.

The bells on the door jingled when I entered and I dropped my red duffel on the floor. I gazed at the row of aquariums. Bubble eyed goldfish swam in circles. I thought it was funny and perverse how we kept fish as pets and also killed them by the ton. Hemingway's *Old Man and the Sea* states, "The fish is my brother, but I must kill him." A bloated goldfish floated upside down.

I looked toward the register. Somebody was doing something behind the desk.

"Hello? Osa?" I called. A girl popped up from behind the counter. Bright, grey-blue eyes and full lips were set on her dimpled, smiling face. An elegant jawline ran past a tiny diamond chin stud. I froze in a sort of half wince.

Did she freeze too?

My head tilted slightly.

"Hi!" I blurted. She tilted her head playfully as well.

"Hello," she said. A pause. "How can I help you?" I stood in paralyzed silence for a few seconds like the goddamn Tin Man whose jaw needed oil. Osa entered from the back door and stood at the girl's side.

"My name is Norris. Hello, Osa," I said.

"I'm Alice," the girl replied, smiling.

Alice! I wanted to say her name aloud.

"My goodness, are you ok?" Osa asked. "You've been through a lot I hear." I nodded.

"I'm ok. Scott's the only one who got hurt," I said.

"What an awful thing to witness," Osa said and shook her head.

"Wait, you were on the *Solstice*? Did you see Scott's accident?" Alice asked. I nodded.

"I'm one of his crew. Well, was one of his crew. It was just me and some high school kids on the boat with him at first," I said. They wanted to hear the story. I needed to tell it.

I told them of Scott spinning in the deck winch and turning off the machine and hailing the mayday.

I told them about the EMT and holding Scott's hand and last I knew he coded twice.

I told them about the chopper and the rescue swimmer and Anthony finding his bloody Spiderman blanket.

I don't remember what else I told them. Osa nodded sagely. Alice stood open mouthed when I fell silent.

"Sounds like you did the best you could. I'm actually an EMT and respond to cases with the Cordova fire department," Alice said.

"Oh yeah? I did ok?" I asked.

"You saved his life, Norris," she said to my discomfort.

"Well, Norris, if you need anything, just let me know. The doors are always open for you," Osa said. She shared a glance with Alice. A small smile played on her lips. "I've got a few things to see to. Can you mind the store?"

"Yup, I've got it," Alice said. Osa walked past me and put a hand on my shoulder. Our eyes locked.

"Anything, ok?" Osa paused in the doorway. "You know, nobody outside of this—" she gestured around her "—is going to get it. Nobody is going to understand how close life, death, victories, and failures are in the circle. It's a fact of life up here."

I understood and could tell she saw it.

"Thanks, Osa," I said as she left. I turned to Alice. "What a great lady."

"Isn't she?" Alice agreed. I glanced at the clock. It was around 1630 hours. "So, how did you end up in Cordova? Where are you from?" Alice asked. She opened a cabinet behind the desk and moved things around while she talked.

"I don't look like a local?" I asked.

"It isn't *that*, I've just been raised here. I'd know who you are by now," Alice said.

"Oh yeah? I'm from Oregon, Portland area," I said. I wandered the store and pretended to look at dog chew bones.

"Yeah? How did you end up here?" Alice asked.

"I'm still not sure to be honest," I said and shared my "I was about to graduate and asked my teachers how to make money" gag. We chuckled and I ended up across the desk from her. "Then I flew up here and pounded the docks for a week. Scott Brown Jr. picked me up and here I am."

"That's awesome. The best kind of adventure is a spontaneous one," Alice said.

"That's so true. I've talked enough. What's your shtick?" I asked. Alice chewed on her lip and looked up to think.

"Well, I live in California now and go to college in Fairbanks. I'm studying biology. But I like to come home for the summers. Once an Alaskan, always an Alaskan I guess," she said.

"California! I was born in the San Francisco area."

"Really?"

"Yup. Ok, this is going to sound kind of random, but you've got to see the Monterey Bay Aquarium," I said. Alice gasped. We talked over the counter, our faces drawing nearer and nearer. The fish tanks whirred.

"I love that place," she said.

"Yeah?"

"*Yes.*"

"My first memory is from there," I stroked my chin. "I remember peering over a seawall at otters in the kelp forest."

"Monterey is gorgeous. I don't think I could live in a place that doesn't have beautiful outdoors. Or an ocean. I try to hike every day."

"I feel the same way. Oregon has got some great stuff, but Alaska sure is something. It's just so big, you know. I saw this t-shirt once that had a to-scale silhouette of Texas tucked into a corner of the outline of Alaska and it said, 'Size Does Matter.'"

"Yeah, I've seen that shirt too. Nothing wrong with messing with Texas. Especially when you're Alaskan," she said.

"With this whole Scott thing, it looks like my fishing season is over. I'm hoping to get up to Denali somehow to go camping. Do you have any tips?" I asked. Alice blushed and looked away.

"I've never been," she said in a small voice.

"What? But you're an outdoorsy Alaskan!"

"I know! It's so bad." We talked about going places and seeing things that nobody else has seen. She told me Cordova EMT stories about people falling through the ice. I told fishing stories, like the one where the *Solstice* ran aground Scott Rock and when Noah almost got squished by the skiff. Alice talked about a dream she had recently. I shared my dream of salmon with people faces. We talked with urgency, like two old friends who bumped into each other at a train station. Were we catching the same train or was hers heading East and mine West? Great merciful universe, by all things sweet and gentle and good and worth living, we talked and laughed until it got dim outside. The solstice was long ago.

She put on her coat.

"Where are you going?" I asked.

"I got off at six and it's almost seven. Where does the time go?" Alice said. She flipped the OPEN sign to CLOSED in the door and turned off the lights. I hoisted my red duffel of dirty laundry over my shoulder.

"Where does the time go? I wish I knew," I said as we exited the store. "Do you live far?"

"Just up the hill," Alice said. She looked at me with big, expectant doll eyes. Even a filthy caveman like me could take a hint like that.

"May I walk you home?" I asked. Alice smiled and my heart doubled in size until it was a jackrabbit in my chest.

"I'd love that," Alice said. We walked up the hill. The sun had set and the road was soaked. Just another summer's day in Cordova. I offered my arm. She took it.

"What is your favorite band?" She asked. I scratched my head.

"Erm, I don't really listen to music," I admitted.

She exploded.

"Don't listen to music? What are you, soulless?" She asked.

I grinned sheepishly and we walked in silence for a moment.

"Deal breaker?" I asked.

"Almost," Alice huffed. We walked past the big fluffy dog, formerly known as the big fluffy puppy, who woofed at us.

"I'm a professional SAR dog trainer, did I tell you that?" She asked. We turned at a bend in the road.

"No, you're just full of surprises, huh?"

"Well, I got to keep you on your toes. You're a tough act to beat though," she said.

"*Pffft*. Do you have a dog?"

"An Australian Shepherd mix who is probably wondering where dinner is," said Alice. We came to a stop by a big wooden house on the hill. It looked like a cousin of Hawk House.

"Aussies are great. So this is it, huh?" I said. Alice turned around and a lock of auburn hair fell over her face.

"I guess so," she said. The air was thick all of a sudden. She half-bit her lower lip.

"Look Alice… I'm really glad I met you. I… well…" I struggled. "Can I have your number?"

"Only if I can have yours," she smiled. We flipped out the phones and exchanged numbers.

"I'll see you again?" I half-asked.

"You could talk me into it," she said and we parted ways. I floated to Hawk House to do laundry and shower. The intellectuals were there, but I don't remember what I said to them. Pete the gossip was keen for Scott updates I didn't know. I was overjoyed to see that Anthony's birthday journal arrived and ran my hand over the Italian leather spin. It was just like mine. Perfect.

I returned to the *Solstice* for the night and invited Alice over text for a salmon dinner, but she politely declined. It was pretty late and I hoped I didn't send the wrong message. I was glad she didn't come, for I burnt the salmon and had to throw out a bag of potatoes. Writhing white maggots had spoiled all ten pounds. I wrote in my journal, "24 hours ago I was holding a dying man and now I'm falling in love."

I slept in and it was glorious. Simple, uncensored glory. I stretched, helped myself to some toast and eggs, and polished off the legendary Joshua Slocum's *Sailing Alone Around the World*. It was a surprisingly dull read for nothing really went wrong. His accomplishment as the first solo circumnavigator aboard a sailboat was an inspiration nonetheless. Strange how that works. Perhaps a relatively dull adventure speaks highly to the wisdom and skill of the adventurer. Maybe this is why we hear more about Shackleton than Amundson.

I started to clean up the cabin and held a bucket of suds and a sponge in my hands when Al and one of his friends entered.

"Hey broheim," I greeted Al.

"Yo man, how's it going? I just forgot my backpack. This my buddy, Lashaun," Al thumbed over his shoulder.

"Sup," Lashaun said.

"Hello," I grinned. Al found his stuff and we hung out for a bit. He was going up to Anchorage with family.

"Are you going to say hi to Scott?" I asked.

"Yeah, I think so. And track down our paycheck," Al said. I was curious as to where our money was going to come from as well, but I hadn't thought about it enough to hunt it down. We bro hugged and Al left with Lashaun. I have yet to see Al again, but had a strong feeling I would someday so that departure from my life was a bit easier to bear.

I cleaned up the cabin and eventually moved to the deck. I hosed everything as best I could before I descended into the fish hold to chuck out bits of seaweed. I heard steps and crawled out to see who it was.

"Noah," I grinned. Noah turned. "How the hell are ya?"

"Oh hey, Norris," Noah smiled and we both entered the cabin. "I'm just getting my raft stuff. Too bad we only had that first day free to use it. Do you need help cleaning up?"

"Nah, there isn't really much to do and I kind of like it. Relaxing, you know?" I said. We quickly found Noah's raft and popped open some iced tea tallboys for a chat. "Yeah, Al was here earlier getting stuff too. He's going up to Anchorage with family. I think he is hunting down our paychecks."

"Yeah? That guy—" Noah shook his head.

"Tell me about it," I said.

"What are you going to do? Finish the humpy season? Go chase some silvers?" Noah asked.

"I don't really know how to go about that," I replied. More fishing was the last thing on my mind.

"Well, Edmond on the *Rikki-Tikki-T* is short crew because Hunter is off to school and I know the guys on the *Quixote*. I think they need a guy. I'll totally recommend you, they are good people," Noah said. This option hadn't really crossed my mind. I was done, going home. I even planned to jog the mile or so out to the ferry terminal that afternoon to grab a schedule, a critical first step in my exit from Cordova.

"Huh," I took a sip. "I'll think about it." We chatted for a while longer until Noah had to go. I said goodbye as a wave of panic settled over me. I assumed my 2008 fishing career was over. My crewmates were starting school, or in the case of Al supposed to be starting school. Scott Brown Jr., captain my captain, was out of commission.

If they are all off the hook, so was I. Right?

I changed into one of my old t-shirts and a pair of shorts to go on a run to the ferry terminal to pick up a schedule. My pace was lamentably slow. Whatever muscle I had gained wasn't in my legs. It was going to be a long couple of miles.

I shuddered and sucked in more cold air. The road to the ferry was an uphill one through Alaskan birch and bright green leaves that dripped crystal raindrops. I gasped up the hill to where the road leveled and the scenery opened. The road hugged the coastline near the lip of an impressive sea cliff and the boom of the waves below helped cleanse my mind. The road sloped downhill. I entered the ferry terminal. I spied a stack of schedule brochures and grabbed one, sweaty but happy.

I could leave tomorrow if I wanted. I thought about the dates and times of departure on my run back. I had to start planning my Denali expedition and call the folks to say I was coming home sooner rather than later. Most importantly, my wolf was out there somewhere.

I stumbled aboard the *Solstice* with my mind made up. I came down from my endorphin rush as I toweled myself off. A shower was my next step. I heard something buzz in the v-berth and poked my head inside to see what it was. My phone danced on the shelf above my berth, its screen alight with an unfamiliar number. I flipped it open and put the receiver to my ear.

"Hello? This is Norris."

"Hello, Norris. This is Edmond Wood, skipper of the *Rikki-Tikki-T*." I nearly dropped the phone and scrambled to shove it back to my ear.

"How are you?" I asked.

"I'm doing fine. Listen, I'm going to be down a crewmember for the rest of pink season and for silvers. Hunter, my skiffman, is starting school," Edmond said.

"Ah, so I've heard," I said and sat down at the cabin table.

"Have you? Good." Edmond spoke in a pleasant conversational tone. We could've been agreeing about what to bring to a barbeque. "I hear you're out of work and I could use you. Are you interested in fishing out the season on my boat?" It was just as I feared.

"No!" I wanted to yell into the phone then smash it into pieces, but my words stilled in my throat. What stopped me? I squirmed in silence. A calm, reassuring voice welled from a place deep inside of me to challenge the desperate plea of the frightened animal of my thoughts.

"Well?" Edmond prodded patiently.

"Can I have a bit of time to think it over? I know you're probably in a rush to nail somebody down, but I need a little time to think and plan. Is that ok?" I asked. I imagined Edmond chewing on his lip.

"Sure, but I need an answer soon. Can you make up your mind by tomorrow?" Edmond asked. I swallowed. The voice in my head got louder.

Just say no, you idiot. Do *you* want to end up in the deck winch this time?

"Yes, I'll let you know tomorrow," I said.

"Great. Call my mother, May. My reception may not be so good. She'll help you arrange a ride on a tender out here to swap out with Hunter," Edmond said. He gave me May's number and hung up. I folded my phone with extra care and placed it on the table.

I sorted through my thoughts and tried to approach the situation rationally. The cons of going on the *Rikki-Tikki-T* included who knew how many more weeks of physical labor and the recently tangible possibility of severe maiming or death. I didn't care about making more money. My $20,000 crew share was more money than I knew what to do with. I put in my time on a highlining boat and the season was almost fished out already. Of course, what of Alice? I didn't have delusions of romantic expertise, but I was pretty sure the heartbreaking breakup happened after the passionate candlelit getting together.

Night came and I thought of Scott Brown Jr. on the deck, his good arm over his eyes and the skipper of the other seiner keeping pressure on his wound. And yet, the calm tide rose within me.

I woke up the next day and reached for my phone to call May. A grandmotherly British voice answered.

"My name is Norris. Your son called me the other day," I said.

"Oh, yes. Have you made up your mind, then?" May asked.

"Yes, sign me up. I'm going. I'll probably develop some kind of complex if I don't," I said.

"Wonderful," May sounded relieved. "That is very good of you. If the horse bucks you off, you have got to get right back on."

"Yeah, I hope whoever thought of that phrase knew what they were talking about," I said. We chuckled.

"Yes, well, there is something to be said about sayings that have endured the test of time," May said. She paused and her voice lowered. "You feel the pull, don't you?" I paused.

"Yes I do," I said.

"Isn't it strange? It is as if there is a big net and we're all swimming along, unaware of how it directs us. Don't you agree?" May said. I nodded. I knew exactly what she was talking about. I thought of my recurring dream, the one with the salmon with people faces.

"Yes. I don't think anybody back home is going to understand what things are like up here," I said.

"They won't, Norris," May agreed, her voice elegant as a royal. "Well, let's get to business. You are going to need a steed to take you to battle."

Return to Sea

I moved off the *Solstice* and stashed a few things like Anthony's birthday journal in Hawk House. May arranged a ride aboard the *Zephyr*, a typical crabber turned tender for the summer. I gathered my backpack-worth of belongs.

I didn't text Alice about my new arrangement. My courage hung on a very thin thread and she had the power to snap it on a whim. I was heading into no-reception territory anyway and tried to move on. She probably wasn't interested in me anyway. Going to sea is in many ways less perilous than rolling the dice with a lover to-be.

The cabin of the *Zephyr* felt larger than most houses with a huge wall-mounted flat-screen TV over a giant table and refrigerator the size of a double berth. I used the head and stood in awe of the walk-in shower. Sure, the work of a crabber on the Bering Sea sounded like hell, but the only boat to rival a crabbing vessel in luxury living on the Prince William Sound were the cruise ships.

I rode in the wheelhouse with Captain Luis, an average-sized, middle-aged man with thinning hair and a boatman's scruff. He was a friendly Oregonian and we talked most of the daylong ride to the *Rikki-Tikki-T*. Also in the wheelhouse was Harry, a great cannonball shaped fellow who was chomping at the bit to join the Marines. TJ was about the same size as Harry but had more ordinary proportions. He was from South Guam and spoke in a Luta accent I struggled to understand, but he laughed a lot and I caught the contagion. We passed rafts of sea otters tangled in kelp beds and grizzly bears on the beaches chewing on salmon. Luis claimed the bears only ate the fatty skin of the fish. To digest the flesh was a waste of calories.

"You shittin' me. They don't eat the meat? That the best part!" TJ talked in his fast Luta accent and roared with laughter. I laughed too.

"Whales off dah the port," Harry said in his slow way. There was an old cartoon I watched as a kid called Baby Huey about a super-humanely strong duckling. Harry sounded like Baby Huey.

"I'm not kidding you, they have to pack on the pounds for winter. Get as fat as possible," Luis replied.

"Are you a bear then?" TJ laughed even harder.

"Hey, watch it," Luis warned gently. He addressed me after a brief silence. "So, this has been you're first season up here, huh?"

"Yeah," I said.

"I hate greenhorns, generally," Luis replied. "One of my best buddies skippered a crabber out of Dutch and put a greenhorn on the hydraulics to break him in. The stupid kid punched the lever the wrong way and *bam* my buddy was sucked into a power block. It ripped him to shreds, splattered all over the deck. That greenhorn kid quit that day and better be living as far from fishing boats as he can, I tell ya what."

I set my jaw in silence for a few seconds.

"We all start out green," I offered. A pause.

"Ain't that a bitch," Luis agreed. The *Zephyr* slowed as a skiff approached us in the dwindling light. "Well, there's your ride. Best get ready." I shook Luis', Harry's, and TJ's hands before I shouldered my pack for my skiff ride to the *Rikki-Tikki-T*. I leapt onto the skiff to see Hunter at the helm.

"What's up, Hunter?" I asked over the motor, but his jolly-slacker demeanor was gone. He was completely focused on the skiff's performance. Hunter didn't respond as we skipped over the water toward the mooring field. His eyes were wide and I could read his thoughts, "It's over, I'm getting the hell out of here if this damned skiff doesn't die on me!"

I made out the blue hull of the *Rikki-Tikki-T* in the waning light ahead of us. She was moored alongside the *Edmond W.* A clean-shaven blonde fellow with an amiable smile met us on the deck of the *Rikki-Tikki-T* and Hunter switched places with the man. I followed Hunter onto the deck. Captain Edmond Wood was there.

"Welcome to the *Rikki-Tikki-T*," Edmond said with a radio announcer's voice and we shook hands. He was about my height with straight, dark brown hair parted neatly down the middle. It was hard to pinpoint his age. His boyish face and patchy scruff suggested twenty, but his calm, mature demeanor begot a person pushing thirty.

"Pleasure to be here," I smiled. Edmond led me into the cabin. Hunter rushed past with a black duffel bag slung over his shoulder and hopped aboard the skiff. The blonde gunned the engine and the skiff disappeared into the darkening evening in a whir of jet wash. They transformed into red and green running lights in the distance.

The *Rikki-Tikki-T* was a little smaller than the *Solstice* but had an inviting open-cabin layout that felt like a living room. The opera masks of Comedy and Tragedy hung on the wall, which I felt were appropriate. I was guided to the v-berth and I stashed my pack. It looked unchanged from when Noah, Al, and I crashed it so long ago in Valdez. It was still much more desirable than a Laundromat floor and this time I had my sleeping bag.

"Come on over to my dad's boat, I'll introduce you to some people. Are you hungry? We have some leftovers if you are," Edmond offered. I followed him onto the deck of the *Edmond W.* The epiphany hit me: Skipper of the

Edmond W. = Charles Wood = Edmond Wood's father. The *Edmond W.* is named after Edmond Wood. I'm a genius.

"Thanks, but I ate on the ride over. Those tenders are a real luxury cruise," I replied. We entered the cabin where a warm scene greeted me. Charles, the old patriarch, and his crew of two lads sat around a table. Pleasant banter filled the air. Charles held a cup of tea, his white hair in a state of professorial disarray. They paused when I entered.

"I present to you, Norris, the new deckhand," Edmond said and waved me front and center. He pointed to each of the guys as he spoke. "I believe you are already acquainted with my father, Charles."

"Charmed," Charles sagely nodded over his tea.

"Likewise," I grinned.

"This is his deckhand, Stewart," Edmond gestured to a lanky college-aged guy with long straight black hair and snakebite piercings.

"Yo," Stewart waved once.

"This is the infamous Beaker, dad's skiffman," Edmond continued. Beaker had curly brown locks and apple-red cheeks under his glasses. He flourished a dramatic bow.

"A pleasure, good sir," Beaker hummed. Charles rolled his eyes and took a sip of tea. The door opened behind me. The blonde who whisked Hunter away entered. Edmond put a hand on his shoulder.

"And this is Paul, our skiffman," Edmond concluded. Paul smiled. We shook hands.

"Hello," I waved to the group and felt a little like the new guy at an Alcoholics Anonymous meeting. "I'm Norris."

And I'm an alcoholic?

"Have a seat, lads," Charles motioned to the table. Edmond, Paul, and I squeezed into the circle. These fishermen had some stories to tell. The *Edmond W.* had caught a sea lion in their seine recently. The furious, bear-

153

sized beast barked hell at them while suspended in the seine above the deck, its jaws snapping and bloodshot eyes rolling. It took all of Charles' finesse with the hydraulics to ease the enraged whiskered animal back into the ocean unharmed. I listened and answered questions that came my way. Beaker turned to me with a friendly smile.

"So, have you been fishing all summer as well?" Beaker asked.

"Yup, aboard the *Solstice*," I replied.

"Oh yeah? What happened with that gig?" Beaker asked.

"Dammit, Beaker," Charles muttered.

"What?" Beaker looked to Stewart for backup. Stewart rolled his eyes.

"Come on dude. The *Solstice*? Scott Brown Jr.? Remember?" Beaker blinked a few times before his eyes popped wide. "There we go," Stewart said.

"Oh," Beaker looked at me before he stood up. "I've got to use the head. Pardon, gents." He bumped his way out of the circle. Edmond and Stewart exchanged a knowing glance. Dammit, Beaker.

The evening was a pleasant blur and I almost forgot how nervous I was. This was a solid group of guys with more endearing quirks than potentially troublesome ones. By the time Edmond excused himself, Paul, and me for bed, I didn't feel like an outsider. I hit my berth hard, the butterflies kept at bay. Tomorrow would be fishing day. Images flashed before my eyes.

Salmon with human faces.

A deck winch under full power.

A hovering Coast Guard helicopter scattering spray.

Once again, I struggled onto the deck through the pure agony of the early morning. The Alaskan summer didn't have much left in it, but this morning was clear enough. The *Rikki-Tikki-T* had an open tophouse instead of an enclosed wheelhouse and I joined Edmond and Paul around the helm. The

Rikki-Tikki-T drifted in the lineup. The sunrise glowed from behind the backs of the mountains.

I was back in the game.

There are many differences in fishing styles from seiner to seiner and it took a couple of days aboard the *Rikki-Tikki-T* to get used to the new setup. Firstly, our power block gripped the seine poorly, much to my dismay. This meant the seine didn't travel through the power block unless I helped it by pulling, so I spent each set doubled over and straining. I imaged a Clydesdale horse at the plow and tried to follow the example. I yielded the results and Edmond complimented my strength. I wasn't used to compliments. They had been sparse aboard the *Solstice*.

We fished near Chenega, a microscopic maybe abandoned town that featured one Russian Orthodox Church at the end of a dirt road flanked by a dozen plywood boxes once called houses. We briefly visited to check the status of a shipment for new gripping for the power block. It hadn't arrived yet.

I was the only deckhand aboard the *Rikki-Tikki-T* and assigned to the cork line. Edmond was content to let the lead line fall on deck in a heap under the power block he manipulated while I flaked the cork line in the traditional piles. Moving from lead line to corks was not a difficult transition, but my stacks were admittedly lopsided for the first day or two.

We fished inside, which meant we were in a crowded bay. The crowd meant rests of an hour or more between sets and time passed easily with Paul and Edmond in the tophouse. I got comfortable enough to recline in the chair and put my feet up. On the first day, Edmond turned to me and spoke in a flawless Sir Ian McKellen's Gandalf impression. *Return of the King*, the last of the epic *Lord of the Rings* phenomenon, was released five years prior in 2003, but was still strong in the zeitgeist.

"Norris, there comes a time for all deckhands when they must act. Will you answer the call? It is time to set the seine," Edmond declared. I leapt to my feet.

"If Gondor calls for aide, the Rohirrim will answer," I said and bounded to the deck, eager to please whatever character he impersonated next. Paul shook his head and smiled on his way to the skiff. Edmond thought aloud in impersonations as well.

"Perhapsh we should shet the sheine outshide today," Edmond mused in a perfect Sean Connery. I tried to imagine a natural conversation between the aloof, conservatively mannered Scott Brown Jr. and eccentric, open-hearted Edmond. The two just couldn't mix in my mind. I got ready for Paul to close up the seine. Edmond burst into deep throated, professional quality opera. There was certainly no mention of the Dixie Chicks.

I reached for a plunger, but Edmond stopped me.

"No need for that nonsense. I'm pretty sure it doesn't do anything," Edmond said. I restrained a jig and passed Paul the towline. I liked this boat.

"Alright Norris, you're on the deck winch," Edmond said like it was no big deal and handed me the purse line. "Here is the switch." He pushed the hydraulic lever up and down, and the winch spun clockwise and counterclockwise. The metallic grinding drained the color from my face. I gazed at the turning machine in a state of hypnosis, the purse line held numb in my hands.

"Is there a problem?" Edmond asked.

Have you seen what this thing can do to a man!? Boots pointed to the sky. The wet crunch of a body. Blue eyes somehow both calm and frantic.

"No," I swallowed and looped a few coils of line on the spinning winch. I leapt back as the winch caught the line. You'd have thought I slapped a sleeping grizzly bear. Edmond's brow cocked, but as long as the line was brought in, he didn't ask any questions. My extra seconds of caution were never brought up. That particular set was a handsome one, but Edmond and I watched a few lucky salmon find the seine's exit under the boat.

"Norris," Edmond sighed.

"Yeah?" I asked.

"You better plunge after all," Edmond muttered and didn't meet my gaze. I tromped over to the plunger and popped it in the water. *Pop!* I hit a few of the salmon on the head, but the fish didn't care and swam to freedom. Plunging felt as useless an ordeal as it ever was, but Edmond relaxed a bit. All skippers are reassured when their deckhands are busy.

Another key difference was the hold. The boat designers, bless them, designed this hold to be free of troublesome nooks and crannies for fish to get caught on, and the hold formed a bowl in the middle where all the salmon collected. It was rare when anybody had to venture into that terrible place to deliver to a tender, or for anything else for that matter. I can think of no reason why all seiners were not designed that way. Clearly somebody on the design team had been a deckhand.

We pulled 44,000 pounds the first day, a fine haul, especially when one thinks about the relatively few sets we put in and the dying season. Instead of shadow puppets and slumber party chitchat in the evenings, we clustered around the modest TV and watched *Smallville*, a favorite of Edmond's and easy watching. Tom Welling's good looks as a young Superman probably played a role in Edmond's fascination.

Paul was the cook and one most prone to bustle about the cabin to take care of housekeeping chores. I glanced over to my captain who sang the *Smallville* theme song under his breath. The opera masks of Tragedy and Comedy hung above him.

"Somebody saaave meee… let your waters break right through… somebody saaave meee… don't care how you do it…" he hummed.

I went to bed surprisingly relaxed and felt my courage begin to return. I was learning the hard way that the adventure seeking of the naïve was not the same as true bravery. Naivety is the first kiss. Courage is the last.

Edmond's eyes shined with manic energy. He gnashed his teeth.

"Another day on the inside. Yesss, in-side," Edmond debated with himself in a Jack Nicholson from *The Shining* voice. His voice dropped and his demeanor turned dark and brooding.

"Yes, yes indeed. Excellent, especially with fava beans," Edmond continued in a Sir Anthony Hopkins' Hannibal Lector. It was another laidback day in a moderately sized lineup with decent weather. We were falling into a smooth rhythm. Paul got better every day as the new skiffman and my cork piles even received compliments from the crew on the tender *Zephyr* when we delivered. The beginnings of the openers were shifted from 0600 to 0700 hours, a development that had me humming merrily for days after I received the news.

"Take the helm for a moment, Norris," Edmond said and left me at the wheel. Scott Brown Jr. never left me at the wheel. I idled in lazy circles at a smooth two knots. Edmond returned with a mug of hot cocoa and watched me.

"Want this back?" I asked.

"You're doing fine," Edmond replied. He taught me a few things about piloting. He taught me all kinds of things I felt like I should've known by now, like how to operate the windlass and hydraulics. Scott Brown Jr. had taken those burdens upon himself, which seemed completely normal when I was his crew. I began to see how unusual that actually was.

No fishing boat can escape Murphy's Law and we had our share of hiccups. The *Rikki-Tikki-T* was not quite as polished the *Solstice*. Hydraulic fluid regularly leaked onto the deck, which was bad news for my Baffin boots.

I nearly fell onto my face half a dozen times and finally realized why everyone wore Xtratufs. I would've given Al quite the show if he were on board. Our refrigerator didn't work, so a typical dinner was pancakes and a stray silver salmon we picked from the humpies in the hold that day.

Edmond sometimes deployed practice sets in between real sets to troubleshoot. Our cork lines kept sinking, but he figured out the cause. I was thankful it wasn't my fault. We typically set around six times and pulled around 15,000 pounds per day. It wasn't a bonanza, but at least we weren't grinding ourselves to a pulp over it.

One day our engine died before an opener. Edmond heaved a musical sigh and crammed himself into the guts of the seiner with a wrench. I hovered near Paul with a worried, thoughtful expression on my face. I felt guilty, but I prayed this was the end. To my inner dismay, Edmond got the engine purring again.

"Ah-ha! A ball bearing was set wrong on the raker." Edmond grinned.

"Nice job, skip," Paul cheered.

"Yeah, nice one," I mumbled. I got into my gear and joined Edmond in the tophouse. He hovered near the *Berserker*, a seiner friend of his, and chatted with the skipper. The *Berserker*'s skipper recognized me.

"I remember you," the man waved a finger at me. I squinted. We had met on the *Solstice*. The *Berserker* must've been one of the seiners that aided us. He was one of the people who kept pressure on Scott's wound.

"How the hell are ya?" I asked.

"Nice to see you back out here, kid," the skipper said turned to Edmond. They resumed their debate about water-cooling systems. We pulled away when it was our turn to set. After we hauled a lousy set, we idled next to the seiner *Scorpio*. The *Solstice* came up again.

"You're the deckhand, aren't you?" The skipper pointed at me. I shrugged.

"I dunno about that," I said. The skipper shook his head.

"You're a goddamned hero, kid," he declared. The two skippers talked water-cooling systems, apparently the hot topic of the day. I had Alice brain and asked Edmond if he knew her after we motored away from the *Scorpio*. He smirked.

"Alice? Yes, we grew up together in Cordova." Edmond paused. "She is completely crazy, but really nice." Edmond coughed. "And not known to slow down relationships." I sighed. Alice had probably forgotten about me and was toying with another fisherman by now. We were about thirty-five cents per pound after all, a real bargain even after the mark up. I gazed at our bow wake and failed to think of something else.

Zombies and a Run to Remember

I knew the fishing season was ending when the zombies invaded.

Salmon stop eating as they mature into breeding stock and start to rot alive if they are late to the spawning grounds. Our sets began to contain more and more of these late arrivals, their hides mottled and scales dull. Hunks of rancid flesh sloughed off their bodies as soon as I touched them. Eyeballs liquefied and fell out of heads. The flesh around the jaw was especially vulnerable. Jagged teeth stuck out at odd angles. My raingear needed regular hosing to get the rotten fish paste off.

Even as the zombies invaded, life was pretty swell aboard the *Rikki-Tikki-T*. The weather was mild and mostly sunny, and the feeling that the ocean was out to kill me continued to wane. The morning of August 28 rolled around and we started the day at a favorite spot on the inside in a six-boat lineup. Edmond idled near the seiner *Parade* and the two skippers conversed. I reclined in my working gear and closed my eyes. It was early, but at least openers were at 0700 hours now.

"Yeah, we're out of here tomorrow," said the skipper of the *Parade*. My eyes cracked open.

"Not a lot left in this run," Edmond agreed. "My dad is probably leaving tomorrow, too."

"A lot are," the *Parade*'s skipper said. I swallowed, the promise too cruel to hope for.

To Morrow!

"Well, I'm up," Edmond saluted and left the *Parade* behind. I rose from my seat and followed Paul to the deck. He continued to the skiff. I readied myself by the release. The boat in front of us was towed clear by their skiff as they wrestled with their catch trapped in the bunt of their seine. Edmond gave me the nod to hit the release.

Clank! Another day of small sets and waiting was away. A boat from the lineup peeled off around noon, no doubt leaving pink season behind for good. I gazed over the water as our seine soaked. Two spouts of vapor and a black fin signaled passing orcas. I sighed and joined Edmond in the tophouse.

"Lots of folks leaving," I said and sat down.

"Not a lot of fish left," said Edmond. "Probably about time to call it quits."

"Yeah?" I floated the question with fake nonchalance. If he told me to take a knee and beg for it, I would've. As far as I was concerned, I no longer had anything to gain out here. I conquered the deck winch and was, blessedly, not afraid of the sea. But I was weary and yearned to be done with this business. Surely, I had passed this test? But no, to beg now would wreck it. *This* was the test, the moment where I either tightened my jaw in resolve to reach the finish line or lost all dignity with surrender. No, as long as there were openers, I would stay.

I had to stay.

"Yup," Edmond said. "I'm about ready to get back to Cordova." He reached for the radio and put the receiver to his mouth.

"Paul, close up," he said. I marched down to the deck as Paul approached and nearly rejoiced at what I saw. Paul struggled to maintain power and an odd clunking rattle came from the skiff's engine.

We hauled in the tiny set and gathered around our wounded skiff-beast. Edmond popped open the cowling of the outboard and poked around with Paul. I hovered on the outskirts and put my hand to my chin like I weighed plausible theories in my head. My brow furrowed, eyes narrowed. If you had been watching me, you would've thought I was on the cusp of figuring out the problem. Instead, my stomach gurgled and I thought of the prime silver we had put aside for dinner.

Edmond righted.

"Well, the gears in the lower unit are messing everything up. We've got to go to Cordova to fix it," Edmond said. He looked around the bay with a satisfied gaze.

"Guess that's it," Paul said.

"Yup, let's deliver and get out of here," said Edmond as he marched to the tophouse.

"Really? That's it? Humpies are done?" I asked in disbelief. Edmond looked over his shoulder with a dashing smile.

"Humpies are done," he said. We promptly delivered and ran through the night back to Cordova. Supplies were low, but Paul managed to compliment the delicious silver salmon dinner with pancakes and green jello. I slept like the dead after an episode of *Smallville* with an ear-to-ear smile on my face.

Blessed Cordova was overcast upon our arrival the next morning. We spent a few hours swabbing the deck and vacuuming the cabin while Edmond installed a new lower unit on the skiff. The only obstacle that remained for me was silver season, which was supposed to be only a day or two long.

Edmond turned us loose around noon and I hustled up to Hawk House with my red duffel bag of dirty clothes over my shoulder. Larry and Pete answered the door. I was spared a Sophie attacked. She must've been with Dora at work or with Darrell somewhere I couldn't guess.

"Norris, my boy," Larry boomed and gestured me inside with a sweep of his arm. "Sisään!" I discarded my boots and threw my laundry into the machine before I joined the two fishermen around the dinner table. Zoe hardly lifted her head. Beers hissed open.

"How'd the pink run finish out for you and the younger Wood?" Pete asked, always nonchalant about potential gossip. I swigged my beer. In that moment the beer was a divine gift from the Gods although it was the same stuff I gagged on a month or two prior. Strange how that works.

"Meh, usually pulled in 15-ers. The gears of the lower unit of our skiff busted at just the right time, I guess. I sure like Captain Edmond though, I can't believe he is only in his twenties. He is so mature," I said. Pete stroked his chin.

"Edmond is nineteen, if I recall correctly," Pete said.

"Nineteen? Wow... that's only a year older than I am."

"Silvers are coming up for you," Larry grinned on the edge of a chuckle.

"Yeah, I can't get my mind around the one-day season thing. How does that work?" I asked.

"Well, silvers are worth 95 cents a pound for one. I guess you've never seen a silver season before," Pete said. His bloodhound eyes shifted to Larry, the more extravagant storyteller.

"It's one big derby, the whole fleet crammed into one little spot. One big set and boom, that boat makes $100k," Larry said.

"Really?" I whistled.

"Somebody usually does," Pete added quietly.

"Wow," I said. We all took a swig of our beers. I swallowed first and changed the subject.

"Have you guys heard anything about Scott?" Larry shook his head.

"Not much, everybody seems to have different intel on the matter," said Larry.

"Word is he coded twice in the helicopter, but he is alive," Pete added. "I heard that he isn't going to keep the arm and things aren't going so well with surgeries coming up. That cat better watch out, that's two lives less and I've heard stories that suggest he didn't have all nine to spare before the season."

"I hear you on that," I said and shook my head. I took another drink. Damn it was good.

"You know his benefit dinner is tonight, doncha?" Larry asked. I shook my head.

"Benefit dinner?"

"Yup, our card-carrying libertarian friend Scott was uninsured," Pete said. "This dinner is meant to raise money for his horrific medical bill. Silent auctions and all that jazz."

"Hmmm... I guess I should be there. Do you know when it is?" I asked. Pete looked at his watch.

"Starts in an hour," he said.

I entered the community building with a grumbling stomach and Anthony's leather-bound birthday journal tucked under the crook of my arm. A few hundred people, a good showing for a town of around two thousand, milled around foldable tables arranged on a basketball court. Family groups shuffled past an impressive donated food spread after buying meal tickets. A row of tables featured goods for the silent auction.

I took a detour and hoped I could afford something. I had yet to receive a paycheck for the summer's work and was afraid to think about the remnants of my high school nest egg. Cans of home-smoked salmon were going for forty bucks a piece, ornate Copper River Fleece jackets for hundreds. The native art-inspired fleeces were an iconic local design, basically the town's uniform. You've probably seen one on Alaskan Airlines staff at the airport. Moose and otter moccasins were not my style, even if I could afford them. Sea otters were still extinct on the Oregon coast from the fur trade. Trophic cascade and all that business bothers me.

I piled my plate high with homemade red-meat-and-potato-style food and spied Noah in a cluster of people. He waved me over. A cherubic cheeked boy of Anthony's age with Noah's dark curly hair sat at Noah's side.

"Noah, good to see ya," I sat down.

"You too man, crazy," Noah nodded. "This is my brother, Jason."

"Nice to meet you," I smiled and shook Jason's hand.

"You too," Jason responded, shy but polite. How different the *Solstice* would've been if Anthony had Jason's demeanor. I took my fork and knife to the meat on my plate and talked between bites.

"How's school treating you, Noah?" I asked.

"It's pretty boring, not gonna lie," he said.

"Yeah?"

"Yeah, it's just so easy."

"Makes sense to me, you're a smart guy. Thinking of college at all next year?" I asked. Noah was, but a career in the maritime industry interested him.

"You know, we were the ones catching the fish, but in a way the fish catch you," he said. We ate leisurely and chatted for quite some time, hours even. The crowd began to thin. We had yet to be recognized as Scott's crew. Nobody seemed to know our role in Scott's chain of survival. Just as well, I reckoned.

"Is this Anthony's present?" Noah asked. He picked up the leather journal I left on the table and flipped through the blank pages.

"You know it. Have you seen the little hellraiser around?" I asked. Noah shook his head.

"He hasn't been in class," Jason piped in.

"Probably visiting Scott in Anchorage," I nodded. "Darn, I'll have to find him after silver season is over."

"You're sticking out the season, huh? How's Edmond as a skipper?" Noah asked.

"He is awesome. I really like working on the *Rikki-Tikki-T*. It's a lot more relaxed than working with Scott," I said.

"Yeah, I get what you mean..." Noah trailed off. We talked until the Feingold clan had to leave. I walked with Noah out the door. We said goodbye in the entranceway.

"It's been good, brother," I said as we shook hands.

"Yeah, you have a place to stay if you need it. I'll see you after silvers are up," Noah said.

"Thanks, I appreciate it. See you soon," I said and waved as Noah and Jason walked across the parking lot. "Bye, Jason."

"Bye!" Jason waved and disappeared in the family car. I thought about going back to the dinner but didn't. I returned to Hawk House for the company and to settle debts. Dora was home from work and I paid her the $300 rent money I owed her. I finished my laundry and joined Dora, Larry, and Pete around the table to get caught up with the world. The 2008 presidential election was gearing up and the golden-boy Barack Obama faced John McCain, the grizzly Vietnam War hero, for the presidency. McCain had just announced Wasilla, Alaska's own Sarah Palin as his running mate that day, August 29. The move sent ripples throughout the country and millions of Americans scrambled to the internet and the news to see what this conservative Alaskan hockey mom Governor was made out of.

"She'll be a force to be reckoned with," Pete insisted. "This kind of gamble is what the McCain campaign needs. They'll lose if they don't mix things up a bit."

"She'll run this country into the ground," Larry declared. "What a load. Has this country already forgotten this awful Cheney administration? Palin, *ugh*!" I reckoned Pete was right. If Palin turned out to be half as eloquent and intelligent as Obama had been so far, McCain could get back in the game. Her first public interviews were going to be important.

I hopped on the computer before leaving to check email and Facebook. I responded to a few friends who wondered if I was alive. I powered on my cell phone for the first time in days and gasped in amazement and horror at the several missed texts from Alice.

"saw you running, wassup? what are you doing later? ☺" kind of messages. My heart soared. I felt physical pain in my gut.

"You fool," I hissed under my breath and texted her back. She didn't respond, so I looked to Facebook. Alice had messaged me that her phone was broken. A green dot hovered by her picture in the chat, so I wrote to her and we got to talking. She was leaving tomorrow, bound for college.

"I'll be running tomorrow. I assume you're taking the ferry? Or the plane? The routes are in opposite directions… I'll have to guess I suppose. If you see someone who needs a haircut running, honk or something. If not, maybe I'll see you in Monterey! Or next summer!" I wrote. She replied.

"next summer FOR SURE i'll be here. and we can keep in touch, my phone should be working tomorrow... so hopefully we can talk… I leave 730 am on the ferry. i'm sorry dear, i don't know that theres time!"

We said our online goodbyes.

I left Hawk House late in the night, my insides empty and my cheeks red from a few drinks and the chill. The big fluffy dog, formerly known as the big fluffy puppy, wasn't on his porch. I shoved my hands in my pockets and hung my head all the way down to the *Rikki-Tikki-T*. The boat didn't charge me rent and I didn't worry about upsetting the Hawk House rooming balance. I hit the berth with a heavy sigh.

My vibrating phone woke me around 0630 hours the next morning. I managed to flip open the display screen. It was Alice. I shot out of bed and texted back, my stomach knotted and heart racing a mile a minute.

"i'm at the terminal," she texted.

The ferry! My thumbs tapped furiously. We shot texts back and forth, "we should've hung out more" kind of stuff. I walked out of the v-berth and looked outside. The morning fog was so thick I couldn't even see town from the harbor. The next text tightened my throat.

"i'm getting on the ferry"

I gazed at the cruel words and their finality. I snapped the phone closed and put my head in my hands. I would've slipped into an unbearably blue mood if it weren't for a sudden heat that consumed me, a fire that would not be quenched until I did something. Out of all the people I met and who faded out of my life without so much as a goodbye, this was the one to fight for. This was the time to rage at whatever it was that trapped me in its seine.

I sprang to my feet a man, not a fish.

"Alice!" I yelled and leapt into my jeans and boots. I bolted out of the cabin of the *Rikki-Tikki-T* and flew over the planks of Old Harbor. Wood groaned under my boots. The sting of the frigid fog goaded me on and I cleared a heap of old line in a single bound. A bearded man straining under a load of gear emerged from the mist in my way. I spun at the last second to avoid colliding with him and tumbling into the brine. I thumped out of the harbor with the sea salt's growling at my heels and hit the road to the ferry terminal.

I would've beaten an Olympian on that run to Alice. The familiar route climbed through the forest until it leveled and turned back to the tempestuous sea. I ran along the rim of the cliff that overlooked the ferry terminal. The waves crashed against the rock below and sent echoing thunder. A foghorn cut the legs out from under me as the ferry pulled away from the terminal below.

I was too late.

"Alice," I gasped and sank to a defeated kneel at the cliff's edge. The ferry cautiously drifted from the dock and into the amorphous gray expanse. The wind rose and whipped my mess of hair across my face. I texted her.

"i see you!" Alice texted back. The ferry idled into takeoff position below. I rose to my feet as rain started to fall. My hair deformed into a wet mane over my face. If this scene played out on the silver screen, a mustachioed ferry captain would emerge, declare his belief in true love, and turn right around with a blow of his triumphant horn. Alice and I would embrace on the dock, she leaping to a straddle around my waist and I holding a fistful of her hair as we breathed hot fire into each other with a deep kiss. The ferry goers would cheer in a raucous chorus and the sun would break as we tore into each other, sinking into a mad tangle of thrashing limbs on the old wood of the pier.

"you don't have to stay there!" Alice's text insisted. I could make out her tiny figure waving on the deck. The ferry's engine started up and crept out of sight.

"Girls make boys do silly things," I texted back. The stern of the ferry vanished into the grey. I stood alone on the cliff with the wind and the waves until my sweat cooled. The wind strengthened and threw the surf against the land with renewed fury. I began to shiver.

I took the long way back to town through the tide zone, my jeans covered in mud and my hair soaking. Barnacle colonies closed and hunkered down in wait for a higher tide. A starfish was prying a mussel open to spit its guts inside and digest the mollusk. Oystercatchers mewled at me and scattered. Tiny speckled sculpins darted in perfect little tidepools. I exposed a feisty crab in a knot of washed-up kelp. A storm was coming. I turned back to my warm berth in town.

We of the *Rikki-Tikki-T* waited out the foul weather by preparing for silver season. The leaky hydraulic panel needed to be fixed, so Edmond, Paul, and I took a pipe wrench to it. Neither Edmond nor Paul could loosen a particularly stubborn bolt.

"It's stuck," Edmond gritted his teeth against the wrench and gave up.

"Let me try?" I ventured.

"Be my guest," Edmond yielded. I spat on my hands and attacked the wrench with a snarl.

"Arrr-gar-rrrarrrg-rar-rrrarrrararw—" I growled and rolled my tongue, my Spanish lessons from high school not completely wasted. Edmond began to laugh.

"What in the world?" Edmond started, bemused. I grunted as the bolt slid loose and I fell onto a knee. Edmond chuckled and he plucked the wrench from my grasp. "Good job," he said.

We steadily crossed items off the *Rikki-Tikki-T*'s to do list. We finally installed new gripping for the power block. My arms wouldn't be exerted to jelly after every set anymore. Better late than never.

"Guess who asked for his job back?" Edmond asked Paul.

"No way… James?" They both laughed.

"You bet, good old James," Edmond said.

"What was James like as a crewmember?" I asked.

"Just awful, the absolute worst," Edmond said. "His attitude sucked and he always complained. The worst part about it was his awfulness infected Hunter. Once James was gone, Hunter shaped right up."

"James seemed pretty confident that he was going to work on Scott Brown Jr.'s boat next year when I talked to him," I said.

"Oh yeah?" Edmond raised a brow.

"I told him Scott won't like that he quit. Scott talked about quitters like they were terrorists or something," I said. Edmond smirked.

"You'll find that James is the butt end of just about every joke we make. James or Beaker, but mostly James. At least Beaker is loveable. I'll certainly never hire the kid again, nor recommend him to anybody." I felt a pang of sympathy for James. He was just seventeen and already carried the mantel of asshole. At least he had a big truck now.

We got ready for the next weather window and the run to Valdez for the silver opener. Edmond and I talked of books. He was delighted to hear I was familiar with Kipling.

"You haven't read *She*? It is aboard for your enjoyment," Edmond declared. "If you like Kipling, you'll love H. Rider Haggard."

"Cool, thanks. *Rikki-Tikki-Tavi* is kind of my inspiration when things get tough," I said. Edmond nodded.

"Read *She*," Edmond said. The time in harbor couldn't pass quickly enough and the cosmic humor struck me. I yearned for the freedom of land when at sea and longed for the adventure of the sea when on land. I nearly laughed out loud when I figured it out. That kind of thing is pretty funny when you think about it.

A Silver Exit

I never saw anything like it before. The whole fleet, must've been over fifty seiners, were crammed in the tiny bay near the entrance of the Valdez harbor during the early pre-opener hours. The civilized rules of the humpy lineups were forgotten, for silver season was derby style that pretty much translated to survival of the pushiest and most cunning. The odds were slim that a second set would do any good, but at ninety-five cents per pound, the potential payoff was huge. One nice bag full of silvers was a fast way to some serious cash. Skippers idled about to get a feel for where to strike. Edmond, Paul, and I took in the zoo from the tophouse on the edge of the action.

"Are we going in there?" I asked, excited. It was impossible not to be excited, and as the clock ticked close to 0600 hours and the opener our positioning would be critical. We all turned at a loud thud to see two seiner captains swearing at each other after a small collision.

"This is nuts," I cackled. Edmond turned the wheel and idled away from the two arguing skippers. Charles and the *Edmond W.* were in the center of the mess, dangerously near the breakwater and harbor channel. Charles was just visible at the helm with his orange Grundens raingear and mane of silver hair.

Balls, man! I thought of Al with a smile. I missed those guys.

"I think we'll work the outside," Edmond said and looked down at his watch. "Get ready, it's about time." No impersonations today. I put on my jacket and clomped to position by the bear trap in my work boots. Paul hopped into the skiff. We were ready for blast off.

I looked at my cork piles.

Pretty cork lines, chief.

An air horn cut through my thoughts.

"Go—" Edmond ordered, but the clanking of machines and the thunder of thousands of horsepower drowned him out. Paul was away into the colorful mess of cork lines that bobbed like the backs of yellow and white sea serpents. Skippers scooped catches by setting right inside rival seines. The only rule was that nobody drove over cork lines, essentially a mutually assured destruction situation. Everything else was fair game. I stared in disbelief as I plunged. Our seine didn't soak for more than a few minutes before Edmond ordered us to close up. We struggled with a nice bag of silvers.

I was in awe of the silver salmon. They were twice the size of the pink salmon on average. The twisted jaws of the males bristled with nasty dinosaur teeth. I was thankful that they didn't try to take bites out of me. Pitching the strays into the hold was more like a brawl than anything, but I was having the time of my life. They fought with many times the vigor and strength of even the largest humpies, and the bigger fish took both my arms to overcome. We hauled in about 9,500 pounds, which translated to around $9,025 for the boat and $900ish for my ten percent deckhand share. Not bad for one set.

I later learned that our numbers were a typical haul. It was certainly nothing to be ashamed of, but the prize for best silver season went to the seventeen-year-old skipper of the *White Wolf* who was filling in for his injured father. The young hero battled into the thick of it near the shore, and when one abnormally courteous skipper asked him which way, right or left, he planned to set, the young man replied, "left." Another skipper asked which direction he was to set, and he told that skipper, "right." This created a wider area to work in, and, instead of setting to the left or right, the young conqueror set against the beach in a half moon formation with the bows of both the seiner and his skiff pointed to shore. By using the beach in such a way, he protected his set from being scooped and took the lion's share of the season.

His was a dashing maneuver that showed both skill and cunning one couldn't help but admire. The word was that each of his crew made $10,000 off one set. Whether or not this was the truth or just dock talk, I never verified. I scanned the action for the *Edmond W.* after the seiners began to disperse.

"Coasties got him," Paul pointed to the rocks. Charles was holding a shouting conversation with two uniformed Coast Guard officers on the breakwater.

"Coasties? Uh-oh," Edmond muttered. The *Edmond W.* had worked too close to the rock breakwater of the harbor and bumped against them. This was a big no-no, rightfully so to avoid oil-leaking shipwrecks. Charles was getting a ticket. The Coast Guard chewed out another skipper who illegally set inside the harbor channel. The two boats lingered like drunks who didn't escape an under-aged frat party busted by the cops. I was with Edmond in the tophouse when a familiar voice spoke over the radio.

"This is Maggie of the *Praetorian* with news of Scott Brown Jr.," Maggie said. I leaned closer to hear. "He is out of the hospital now, although his battle has just begun. He requires seven more surgeries, but it looks like he will be keeping his arm. He may be back in Cordova as soon as next week. Please keep him in your thoughts and prayers. Out."

I took a deep breath and let a wave of emotion wash through me. I was happy Scott was alive, amazed he was going to keep his arm, and anxious about seeing him again. A chorus of "Good to hear," followed from just about every boat on the channel.

"Whew," I took a deep breath.

"Was she and Scott…?" Edmond asked nonchalantly.

"Definitely," I said. We motored into Valdez and met with the crew of the *Edmond W.* at a restaurant called The Totem. The place was the typical Alaskan diner with a kitschy wood-cabin feel and fishing gear on the walls. Charles excused himself shortly after the two crews settled around a large roundtable.

"I have a date with the Coasties," Charles announced and flourished his ticket.

"See you in a few hours," Edmond said. I got comfortable in my seat and reached for a lunch menu. We were going to be here for a while.

"Well, one nice thing about a date with the Coasties is that you know you're going to get fucked. Ta!" Charles bid us farewell and the group settled into warm, pleasant banter. Just about all of us got a proper burger, a symbol of the best of what civilization had to offer. I was surprised to hear May Wood was ill and hospitalized in Providence Hospital in Anchorage, the same place treating Scott Brown Jr.

"Do they know what's wrong with her yet?" Stewart asked. Edmond shook his head.

"No, but her skin is turning yellow. Some kind of hepatitis, maybe?" I thought of the pleasant voice on the other end of the phone and chewed my burger thoughtfully. I didn't know what to say.

We tried a set the next day, but all we caught was a few hundred pounds of zombies. Most of them fell apart in a mush of rank, pale goo when the seine pulled them aboard. I picked one up from the deck. The middle of the fish sloughed off and landed between my feet as a sort of jelly. I wrinkled my nose and rubbed the fish residue from my gloves onto my rain pants. Edmond watched me and turned back to the tophouse.

"I guess there are no more fish to catch," Edmond mused and set course for Cordova. I desired this moment for so long, but when it happened I felt empty. I hosed the rotten fish smears off my raingear for the last time.

I wasn't completely off the hook in Cordova for there was plenty of tidying up to do aboard the *Rikki-Tikki-T*. Paul and I spent several mornings and afternoons on our knees armed with brushes and Simple Green cleaner. Edmond promptly left for Providence Hospital in Anchorage with Charles to see to May, but Paul must've been left with the to do list for he knew what general maintenance stuff needed to be done. I ventured into the hold to remove rotting gobs of black and green goo. Paul reprimanded me for not wearing gloves. Apparently, there was a high risk of infections and parasites. Lovely.

We usually took lunch together at Baja Taco, one of the few eating establishments in town. The kitchen was a renovated school bus parked next to a shack with an undoubtedly colorful backstory I regret not investigating.

I schemed during the evenings, either at the computer of Hawk House or over my journal. My Denali plan started to come together and I reserved a train ticket from Anchorage to the stop at the Denali National Park entrance. It was the last passenger ride north for the season. I hoped to wrap up my Cordova commitments before the date. The fast ferry was to be my ride out of Cordova, but it was going to drop me off in Whittier, a few hours' drive south of Anchorage. I needed somebody to take me from Whittier to Anchorage, and the piece to the puzzle fell into place perfectly when I decided to visit Jane's Knives, a small outdoor store in Cordova's downtown.

My schemes demanded suitable camping gear, namely a tent and a stove. I also thirsted for the perfect knife. How I got through a whole season as a fisherman without my perfect knife was beyond Paul's understanding.

"Carrying a badass knife everywhere is one of the perks of being a fisherman!" Paul insisted, a sentiment I didn't expect to hear from the mild mannered skiffman. He quickly convinced me that I wasn't a complete fisherman without one. I immediately felt emasculated. Men can be silly, but it sure as hell is fun to be one.

No more! I vowed as I entered Jane's Knives.

"Welcome to Jane's Knives," a short robust woman with hair dyed so light it was almost white sprang at me. She smiled an impossibly wide, honest smile with a gap between her two front teeth. Her skin was tan, almost orange. She wore a zip-up hoodie that showed a tad much of her mighty cleavage. Her jeans were a size too snug. Buxom and bubbly were two words that came to mind.

"You've got to be Jane. Nice to meet you, I'm Norris," I said.

"Sure as shit am. How can I help you, dude?" Jane asked. A middle-aged man with a mustache and thick glasses of 1980's vintage coughed from behind the counter. "That's Derrick. Say hi, Derrick," Jane called over her shoulder. Derrick was reading an old issue of *Guns and Ammo*. He raised a silent palm in greeting while his eyes remained transfixed on the magazine.

"I'll be doing some backcountry camping in Denali and I need a few things. I also thought I'd check out your knife selection. I don't have a good knife right now," I said. Jane's eyes gleamed.

"Follow me," Jane said. She jogged behind a display table that ran the length of the room. I beheld a staggering array of blades.

"What kind of knife were you thinking of? We've got brand names like Benchmade," Jane said and flipped out a knife with spring assisted opening. *Snap!* The shining little blade locked into place and pointed at me. Jane flipped it back. "And Kershaw. We've got serrated and non-serrated edges." Jane ducked behind the display case and emerged with a knife the size of my forearm. "We've got Bowie knives. Check out that sexy antler handle! We've got machetes, great for taking on the bush." Jane disappeared again.

"I didn't know there were so many kinds," I began. Jane emerged with a katana.

"Pretty badass, am I right? Right?" Jane cackled.

"That is really cool," I said. I knew a small serrated knife made sense for cutting line, while something big and sharp would probably be better for my Denali experience. I tried to think of a good reason to buy the katana but couldn't. Denali wasn't known for its ninjas.

"I better think a little more about what I'll need the knife for and then get back to you. Do you have tents and camper stoves?" I asked. Jane looked slightly deflated but perked up and turned to Derrick.

"We've got some of that shit, don't we?" Jane asked.

"What's your plan, son?" Derrick asked and furrowed his brow.

"I'm going to do some solo camping in Denali—"

"You're not going to pull an idiot move like that *Into the Wild* jackass, are you?" Derrick gave me the old once over.

"No, no, I'm only planning on a couple of days and I'll be prepared for it," I countered. "He was more ambitious and was going to try to live out there."

"Good, cause that idiot got what he deserved," Derrick said. I bristled inside. I still hate it when people throw Chris McCandless under the bus. Was the guy idealistic and unprepared? Certainly. Did he deserve to slowly starve to death alone in the wilderness because he chased a different kind of life? No. No, damn it, no and no again. A part of me thinks the threat of McCandless' potential success at living a peaceful, less materialistic life is the real reason a certain type of person enjoys the story of his fall. It only takes one idealist to succeed for the small-hearted people of the world to hate themselves. I shrugged it off.

"I'm leaving on the ferry, but I'll need a ride to Anchorage from Whittier. How do people do that?" I asked. Jane interjected.

"We're taking my truck over that way ourselves next week. You can hop on, no problem." We compared days and it lined up perfectly. I'd get into Anchorage the day before my train departed. I agreed to pony up $25 for the lift. We shook on the deal. I turned to Derrick.

"Got a tent? Camping stoves?" I asked.

"You bet, come with me," Derrick said and led me to the back. His tent was a giant Army surplus monstrosity missing a rain fly. I doubted it would even fit in my backpack. His stoves were all large Coleman double burners, again unsuitable for backcountry work. I left Jane's Knives without buying anything, but at least I was all lined up for Denali. I just needed to wrap things up in Cordova and collect a few checks.

Paul announced that May was diagnosed with terminal cancer and Captain Edmond wasn't coming back. He also had the number of the Iverson's, the family who actually owned the *Rikki-Tikki-T*, and I was to get in contact with them about my check. Paul and I had a final lunch at Baja Taco after doing our last chores and parted ways, he destined for Seattle and school.

I said a lot of goodbyes that week, for everyone was hustling to tie a bow on the season and head home. Most of the fishing labor force did not live in Cordova year-round, Paul of Seattle and I of Lake Oswego being textbook examples. Post-fishing season Cordova was consumed with a relieved, hushed urgency. I was not the only one scurrying about town with to-do lists and schemes.

I enjoyed Kara and Zach's company at the free annual dinner hosted by Trident Seafoods, the corporation we all delivered to, in the Reluctant

Fisherman Inn. Kara and Zach had a strong finish on their boat, but I still netted more than them overall. Kara's boyfriend had a devil of a season as the green guy on a boat of snarly old sea salts. But we all made it to the end. We eagerly planned a final barbeque that never came to fruition.

I spent my final nights in Hawk House with the intellectuals. A room was open and Dora left me a peach and a note to walk Sophie every morning. Debbie already left to teach English, but Larry strutted large at our final meal together as the highliner of the radio group. He made a killer lasagna for the group's sendoff and put me to work on salad duty.

This was the last night the radio group would be together until next season. Dora, Pete, Darrell, and a few other fishermen I didn't know gathered around the table. One of the unfamiliar faces was a bear of a man named Buck who wore two sets of glasses, "one for readin' and one for seein'."

"Do you have a ride for the ferry tomorrow, Norris?" Dora asked. I swallowed my mouthful of heavenly lasagna.

"No, I figured I'd just walk. It isn't that far—"

"Nonsense," Dora insisted and we hammered out the driving logistics. I have yet to meet a soul kinder than Dora's. The night darkened and the fishermen told tales of the sea under the glow of a single ceiling light.

"Orcas are the smartest damn animals there are. No offense, fellas. And no offense, Zoe," Larry winked at the wolf-like dog in her corner. Buck thumped the table.

"I knows a guy, longliner, who had the hardest time with those things. They just swam up and down his hooks, enjoying the all-you-can-eat buffet," Buck said as he peered over a pair of his glasses, the ones for readin'. "So my buddy has got a buddy on another longliner, and they gets together and hatch a plan. One guy puts out his line, and when the killers come, he pulls his line in real fast. While the killers are distracted, the other guy puts out his line a few miles away. When the killers go to him, the first guy pulls in his and the other guy gets to fish again. And so it goes. But them killers—"

I had moved from red wine with the lasagna to beer. Dora quietly served each of us a bowl of mint chocolate chip ice cream.

"Thanks," I whispered as I accepted mine. Buck leaned over the table.

"—but them killers, they get tricked for a few hours, but they gather in a big group between the fishermen. My buddy scratches his head and gets back to fishing. Well, he swears the killers talked to each other, because they split up." Buck gestured with his hands. "Half of them camp out under my buddy's boat, half of them under the other guy's. They still got their buffet!" He thumped the table. The fishermen shook their heads in disgust and admiration while they sipped their wine glasses. "Shit, that's what I would've done if I was a killer," Buck said.

The party dissipated until it was just Larry, Pete, and I. Palin's momentum died after she opened her mouth on public TV. Larry was gleeful. We all turned on the news to watch Hurricane Ike slam into Galveston, Texas. I had an uncle who lived there and we all worried.

I met Amy Brown at the *Solstice* to collect my check later in the week.

"How is he?" I asked after we drew away from our hug. I was eager to cross reference the optimistic words of Maggie of the *Praetorian* and the pessimistic ones of Pete the gossip. Amy beamed.

"He is doing much better now. I'm not sure what you've heard, but it looks like he is going to keep the arm," she said. I sighed with relief. Score one for Maggie.

"That's great to hear. There are all kinds of stories flying around," I said.

"Welcome to Cordova. Anthony is back in school now, but Scott will be in Anchorage for a while longer. The two boys were adorable, just about inseparable in Anchorage. Scott thanks God almighty every day for his mercy and is rearing to get back to his real life here. He is planning to fish next year," Amy said proudly. I shook my head.

"Sounds like Scott," I said. Amy reached into her purse and handed me a folded piece of paper. I unfolded a $15,000 check.

"Holy f—"

"I know it isn't all of it," Amy interjected. "But you'll get the rest of it when Scott gets his records in order. I'm sure you understand the circumstances."

Amy studied my face.

"You ok?"

"Y-yes. I'm fine, thank you," I said and stuffed the treasure in my jean pockets. Until that point, I'm pretty sure my largest check was $200 for painting the interior of a family friend's restaurant.

"You've earned it. Scott told me he had a heck of a crew," Amy said. "Hope to see you again."

"You too, thanks for everything," I said. Amy turned to leave. "Wait," I stopped her. "I'm planning on passing through Anchorage on my way to Denali to do some camping. Would... it be ok if I... visited him?" Amy nodded vigorously and took out a piece of paper from her purse.

"Of course, I bet he'd love that," Amy said and pawed herself for a pen. I always carried one and handed her mine.

"Thanks." She scribbled down an address. "He is staying with his sister, Stacy. It's near the hospital for the surgeries he is going to need."

"Thank you so much. I'll call ahead when I know more details," I promised. My phone buzzed. Amy left and I answered it. It was Mrs. Iverson.

"Hello, this is Norris," I said.

"Hello, Mr. Comer. I have a check for you here. It isn't everything we owe you, but you'll get the rest once Edmond gets his records in order. I'm sure you can understand the circumstances. Can I meet you to hand it off?"

"Certainly, I understand. Cancer? How awful."

"Yes it is," said Mrs. Iverson. We hovered on the phone in silence for a few heavy seconds.

"How much is the check?" I ventured.

"$4,000," Mrs. Iverson replied. I put my hand to my mouth and cussed. Just like that, I was $19,000 richer. Lil Wayne dropped the song *Got Money* a few months earlier and I'll admit it popped into my head.

The first thing I did with my money was upgrade my beaten-up wardrobe. I purchased one of the black hoodies I had seen fishermen wearing around the docks. The hoodie featured a picture of a seiner running through nasty chop under the giant words "Alaskan Fisherman." I figured I earned the varsity jersey and it immediately became my go-to hoodie for years.

I also bought a Copper River Fleece, a green and black long sleeve. Tribal designs of salmon adorned the shoulders. Unbeknownst to me, the design was created by the very Mike Webber who lamented his poor herring boat settlement from the oil spill to the *Seattle Times*. The fit was trim and perfect. I could finally pass as a Cordovan and look damn fine while at it.

Only one task on my list remained. I marched to the local middle school with Anthony's birthday present in hand. Noah met me to act as my guide, for it simply wouldn't do for an unknown ruffian like me to invade an elementary school on a boy hunt. Noah's brother Jason went to school there and he knew the lay of the land. We timed our visit in the afternoon, around the time when kids would be milling about after class.

"There he is," Noah singled out Anthony from the herd in the school hallway.

"Hey, Anthony!" I called and we made our way to him. Anthony spun around. A mischievous grin spread across his face. He leaned under his backpack and ran for it.

"God damn it," Noah muttered.

"Anthony!" I called and took off after him past lockers and wide-eyed school children. We rounded a corner. Anthony was trapped against the wall, his eyes shifting for an escape. "Gotcha," I chuckled and loomed over him like I was about to whomp him. His birthday present was hidden behind my back. Anthony's eyes widened.

"What is it? What do you want?" Anthony asked nervously. I leaned in with my biggest smile and handed him the leather-bound journal.

"Happy Birthday, Anthony!" I cheered. Anthony opened it, hundreds of blank pages for him to fill as he chose. I scribbled on the inside of the cover in my abysmal handwriting; *This could be the best story in the world, you only have to write it.*

A Tour of City Curbs

Stepping onto the Chenega fast ferry was a thrill. Not only was the vessel a marvel, a giant floating rocket ship that threatened to fly off the water, but I was completely free for the first time since I arrived in Alaska. I was no longer married to a fishing boat or constrained to the small, but lovely, borders of Cordova. The fast ferry reached her thirty-five knots of cruising speed and I conquered mile after mile of Prince William Sound without doing anything.

I wandered forward and sat next to a tall man with long matted hair and a mostly blonde beard. A backpack, the old school kind he might've gotten at an Army surplus store, sat at his side. He wore faded water wicking pants, a beat-up protective shell layer, and a heavy pair of filthy hiking boots. I eased my embarrassingly clean pack at my feet and brushed something off the shoulder of my new fleece. We had the best view in the house and beheld nature's glory.

"Fisherman out of Cordova?" I ventured to ask.

A pause.

"Cannery worker," he replied.

"Oh yeah? How was that gig?" I asked.

"Sucked," he said. "Sasha." He offered his hand.

"Norris," we shook. Turns out, Sasha had quite a tale to tell. He worked in a Cordova cannery, perhaps processing the pink salmon I caught, before he struck out across the Sound in a rubber inflatable dinghy with a bunch of animal traps. The plan was to build a settlement and trap enough animals to survive the winter alone in the wilderness. Sasha didn't trap enough and made the wise call to abort his plan before it was too late. Even his exit was harrowing.

"It was a pretty long row back to town and the weather was god-awful. So, I'm shivering and rowing for miles with the last of my supplies on board and the sea lions got wind of me. They circled the boat and keep trying to get at my supplies. I was fighting them off with my paddles," Sasha said in a calm, quiet voice. I could picture the scene, the angry puffs of sea lion breath and the shifting whirlpools of flippers and whiskers. Sasha fell silent and we continued to jet through fjord landscapes under clouds only an artist could recreate. The interior of the ferry was white and sterile. We might as well have been abducted by aliens.

"Where are you from, Sasha?" I asked.

"New York," he said.

Jane took a liking to Sasha and agreed to take him with us to Anchorage. Sasha and I put our backpacks in the bed of her truck and we began the road trip on AK-1 from Whittier. Rain was coming. Sasha's pack looked waterproof. I put a garbage bag over mine.

Derrick sat in the passenger seat next to Jane, who was a talker the whole way. She had all kinds of stories, like how she used to poach elk in some desert state of the lower forty-eight. She once slipped an elk kill right under the nose of a highway patrolman who stopped to question her off-road. He knew of her, flirted with her a while, and sent her on her way, the bloody carcass stuffed barely out of sight across the truck bed. We drove past

Turnagain Arm and below us shimmered the tidal flats newly exposed at low tide.

"You watch yerself if'n you ever go down there, oh boy," Jane said and shook her head. "There's quicksand out there, make no mistake. The other year there was a newlywed couple that took some four-wheelers out there onto those flats at low tide. They got stuck in the muck, and when they tried to walk back, the muck got a hold of them too. Then the tide rose and they were goners."

"Jesus, Jane," Derrick said.

"What? It happened," Jane's voice cracked, her smile with a gap between the two front teeth still wide on her face. "Belugas live down there too. This one time—"

Forests and ocean views gave way to two-story houses and mailboxes as we drove into the suburbs of Anchorage. We arrived at Scott's sister's house. I was dropped off on the curb.

"Good luck, dude," Jane saluted. Sasha and Derrick nodded once in farewell before Jane of Jane's Knives motored out of my life forever. I adjusted my straps and walked up to the door. I bit my lip. What would I see in the Brown household? I worked my jaw to loosen it up and knocked. A blonde woman who looked a few years shy of thirty with full kiss-me lips answered.

"Can I help you?" She asked from the partly open door.

"My name is Norris and I'm—" I started, but she threw the door wide open and beckoned me inside.

"Come in, I know who you are. I'm Stacy, Scott's sister. Your timing is perfect. He was sleeping before. Scott! Look who's here."

Stacy led me deeper into the house. We entered a white, high-vaulted living room. Captain Scott Brown Jr. sat on a long couch in front of a large TV screen. His right arm was an L of rigid plaster propped on a chest-high pile of pillows at his side. Scott turned his icy blues on me. His pale face was haggard with wrinkles and bruises. My eyes began to well.

"Scott—" I began.

"Norris, I promise I'll get you the rest of your money soon," Scott Brown Jr. cut me off. My mouth hung open, ready to complete what I started to say.

Scott, I'm so happy you're alive.

"I promise, Norris," Scott said again, an earnest tinge in his voice.

Damn the money, Scott. Damn it, curse it. I hate it! I wanted to scream.

"You'll get paid what you worked for," Scott insisted.

"Don't worry about that. It's not why I'm here," I said. I swallowed and put my pack down so I could sit with him. I don't remember where Stacy ended up, but she left us alone.

"I know you're good for it. I'm just passing through the area and thought I'd drop in is all. I'm heading up to Denali," I said.

"Ah," Scott Brown Jr. said and fell silent. I couldn't tell if he was on painkillers, still sleepy, or just being his aloof self. Probably all three. I glanced at the TV screen. A sexy woman with a bunch of guns was getting eaten alive by large bugs on the Sci-Fi channel.

"How are things?" I nodded toward his arm.

"It looks like Frankenstein's monster under there, all stitched to shit and all. I'm in physical therapy now," Scott said. He wiggled a few fingers to prove it and winced. "Hurts like a motherfucker though and itches like crazy."

"Yeesh, I'm amazed they saved it," I said.

"Yeah, it is pretty crazy what they can do these days," said Scott. We fell silent and gazed at the TV. The CGI bugs were on a rampage eating more attractive people.

"What the hell is this?" I asked.

"I have no fucking clue," Scott said.

189

We sat like that for a good while to burn time until the Browns could give me a lift to Providence Hospital. Scott had an appointment and I was going to visit May Wood. Timing couldn't have been better. I unsuccessfully tried to bait Scott into a proper conversation every once in a while. There was a part of me that wanted, no, needed to talk about that day at sea. Did you remember me holding your good hand as you gritted your teeth against the reaper? Did you see anything on the other side or was there nothing there as I suspected? Of course, these things didn't come up. No sane person would go there. The glass surface of the pond was not disturbed and so the depths beneath remained unexplored. We were left with only our reflections to gaze upon.

"Got any plans for next season?" I ventured.

"Yup, I'll be out there fishing. I'll need to hire additional crew to help out, though," Scott said. A melancholy, but proud, grin played on my lips. Scott Brown Jr. was no quitter, for better or worse.

"The benefit dinner for you was really something. Half the town was probably there," I said.

"Yeah, I'm still pretty far in the red ink though," said Scott.

"Yeah?"

"Yeah." We fell silent as I fully transformed into a Medicare For All supporter. It is some kind of disgusting that hard-working folks like Scott get wiped out like that in the land of the free.

Stacy joined us and I ended up mostly talking to her. She planned to work on the *Mantis* next year and was getting an education degree in the meanwhile to be a teacher. I piled in the back of Stacy's car for the ride when it was time to go.

Again I was left at the curb, this time at Providence Hospital by Stacy and Scott who exited my life unceremoniously like just about everybody else. It stopped raining, so I took the wet garbage bag off my pack and stuffed it into an outside pocket. I walked into the lobby of the hospital after I adjusted my straps and followed directions from a directory up an elevator to Emergency Care. The sterile white interior reminded me of the fast ferry. I wandered the halls in circles, unsure of what May Wood looked like. I passed room after room of bedridden, mostly older folks in hospital gowns. They were hooked up to monitors and machines that whirred and beeped and spat out numbers. Sometimes the patients were asleep. I was often the target of sad, vaguely hopeful gazes from behind nasal cannulas. I kept walking, nervous to stop and risk becoming bedridden myself.

"A Cordovan," a chipper British accent called to me. I turned around to see an older lady in a hospital gown beckon, a nurse on one side and a younger blonde woman on the other. The older lady leaned heavily on a walker. "I'd recognize the patterns of that fleece anywhere."

"Are you May Wood?" I asked as I approached.

"You must be Norris! How great to meet you at last," May beamed and reached out an arm, the offering for a hug. I gave her my best. Her skin had a yellowish tinge to it and her tawny hair seemed thin and dead on her skull. The nurse carried a wheeled stand with an IV bag. The plastic tube snaked up a sleeve of May's hospital gown.

"It's so great to meet you too," I drew away.

"I'm Marge," the blonde woman said. We shook hands.

"I'm Norris. I was a deckhand for May's son this season," I said.

"And he was with Scott Brown Jr. on the day of his accident," May added. "Oh, Charles and Edmond have said such nice things about you," she gushed.

"They did? Lies, I assure you," I joked. May chuckled. She had a rich laugh, a sound so wonderful and genuine I couldn't help but join.

"Mrs. Wood, let's get you back into your bed," the nurse prompted. May began to shamble down the hall. I walked with her, a man in the spring of his life and a woman in her winter.

"So, what do they have you in here for?" I asked. May ho'ed and hummed.

"Well, they're not really sure, but it is some kind of liver, pancreatic cancer combination or what have you," May said. Her gaze was directed down to mind her walker. She breathed heavy. "I already said no to chemo. You see, I always promised Edmond that we would go to the Italian Opera, and by Jove we're going to go." Another nurse approached with a wheelchair. May eased into it. "It has been too long since I've been to Europe… whew, thank goodness." May melted into the seat and her eyelids drooped. "I'm exhausted." Marge stepped forward.

"I should probably go and let you rest. I'll see you soon, ok darling?" said Marge. She leaned down and hugged May, who patted her shoulder.

"Oh, dearie me, I've kept you all day," May sighed.

"It was wonderful, don't you worry," Marge said and pulled away. I took my cue.

"I better leave you to rest up for Europe," I said and hugged May goodbye. She touched my elbow.

"It was such a pleasure to meet you. I'm so glad this happened," May said. I drew back. May was wheeled into her room.

"Me too," I said. Marge and I walked into the elevator and stood in silence as we descended. "So, how does it look? Is she—"

"They gave her a couple of months, tops," Marge said quietly. She sniffed and wiped a tear out of the corner of her eye. I worked my jaw to speak but couldn't think of what to say. The elevator stopped with a lurch and opened.

"Is it always like this around here?" I blurted as we stepped out of the elevator and walked into the parking lot. Marge wiped her other eye and looked at me levelly.

"Yes, I suppose it is," Marge said. I asked her for a lift to the mall. I had one more group of people I wanted to see.

I was dropped off on yet another Anchorage curb. It was a drab scene of asphalt roads and grey concrete buildings drowned in a chill downpour from overcast skies. My patterned fleece whisked the rain into glassy beads and my beanie kept my long hair from getting completely soaked. I left the drone of cars behind and made for the nearest overhang near the mall's entrance. I paused to get my bearings under the shelter and mentally prepare for my assault.

"Jerry. God damn it, Jerry. Jerry!" A middle-aged man dressed in a business suit yelled to the left of me. I started and nearly told him that I was not Jerry, but stopped when I saw the Bluetooth device in his ear. Those things weren't too common back then. Like the iPhone, I was pretty sure it was a fad.

"Jesus. Lord Jesus. Jesus!" A disheveled man with wild brown hair shouted to my right. He wore a tan winter coat, the kind of hand-me-down an Alaskan tramp would need to get by. His teeth were yellow or missing, his skin wrinkled to suggest an elderly age, but who knew? I took a deep breath and left the two madmen. I was to find the Wood men in the food court.

I entered a world of hard light and tall ceilings, a glowing warren that echoed the collective rumble of thousands of mall goers. A flawless woman walked by, her full lips red with lipstick and perfume so heavy I was struck stupid. A little girl led her dad by the hand to a window where a robot dog shuffled back and forth. An absurdly muscular man checked himself out in the reflection of a clothing store and puckered his lips. An overly friendly woman with brown hair emerged from a booth and tried to sell me a smartphone case. I opened my mouth to speak, but words didn't come and I marched on after a frustrated sigh. I hadn't seen such a stream of faces since my dreams of salmon people.

I navigated my route to the food court and spied the two captains, father and son, seated around a table. How small and out-of-place they looked, hunched over gyoza platters and dressed as urbanites. They belonged in raingear behind the helms of great metal boats taking on Alaska's oceans. Seeing them in the food court as one of the mall-going salmon-people was like seeing Santa emerge red-eyed from a strip club or Superman crying in a tutu.

I greeted them and they welcomed me with small smiles and quiet, friendly greetings. There wasn't too much to say. I'm not even sure if May came up, even though she was the common reason we had of visiting Anchorage. We wandered in circles for an hour or so. Edmond bought caffeine pills and got an expensive haircut. My hair cut was long overdue, but I chickened out and didn't cut it.

The time came to depart and find Edmond's car, the "Skippermobile", but the two skippers had no sense of direction. Soon we became lost. I consulted a mall map and took charge. I led them to the parking garage.

"C'mon guys, it's just like navigating the sea," I laughed. Charles muttered something clever and at my expense. They whisked me to the train station. The two fellows gave me an unsentimental farewell on the curb by the tracks and vanished into the night.

Follow the Hawk's Cry

I sat under the glass ceiling of a mostly deserted car of the Denali Star's last passenger ride north. The upgrade to Gold Star Service was $85 and I splurged. What was $85 to a fisherman after payday? Miles upon miles of stunted birch and alder flaunted gold, red, and brown leaves announcing the incoming fall. An endless patchwork of lichens made up the living quilt of the taiga. There was no ocean where I was steaming. A young lady wearing a navy conductor's jacket and hat approached me.

"Excuse me, would you like a drink?" She asked sweetly. "No charge."

"No charge? Really?" I asked, suspicious. She smiled.

"It's included in the Gold Star ticket, I promise. You didn't pay more money just for the view."

"In that case, I'll take a ginger ale," I said. The train lady left. I caught the eye of a little blonde girl seated with her family. She must've been about six and peeked at me from behind the corner of her chair. Her face broke into a big, chubby smile that lacked a couple teeth. I made a goofy face at her and she disappeared in a fit of giggles. Kids are great.

The train lady returned with my ginger ale. I asked her about working on the train. It seemed like a pretty laidback way to earn some cash and see lots of Alaska. She said she liked it but perked up when we got on the topic of what I had been doing for the summer.

"Oh, I want to do that so bad," she said. She went to picking my brain, but I didn't have much energy for it. "You made how much?!" Kind of stuff. To be honest, I didn't really want to encourage her. I thought of those grinder days and how close we worked to serious injury. I thought of this nice train girl in a deck winch and shuddered.

She went about her business and I took to gazing at Alaska. We floated past a beaver dam the size of a gillnetter. It was a pile of sticks worthy of a witch burning. We approached the entrance to Denali and a growing part of me dreaded my stop. Life was so easy as a Gold Star rider complete with train ladies pampering you and miles of wilderness passing without effort. Honestly, I just about threw up when the train ground to a halt. I tightened my straps, my first night of camping ahead of me.

The sun was setting and I missed the local camping supply store's hours. The store's closure meant I had no tent for the night, and I kept a wary eye to the overcast September sky as I found a campsite at the Denali campground. It was an unexciting campground with sites jammed up next to each other in a scrubby forest. I resolved to sleep on top of the picnic table at my plot and move underneath in the likely occurrence of rain. The first step of my plan had been to visit the rental store. Without the visit, I was missing some very important things. I didn't have any materials to start a fire and didn't even attempt any stick-on-stick business.

I turned at the sound of approaching footsteps and beheld a forty-something-year-old Asian lady. She wore a long-sleeved blue fleece that looked like the REI tag had just been cut off. The lady smiled at me behind thick frame glasses.

"Are you hungry? Wan food?" She spoke in a heavy Chinese accent. I uncoiled from my half-crouch and tried to unwind my worried frown into a smile. The woman, bless her, didn't waver despite my vaguely feral aura.

"It is Moon Festival. We have food. For you," she beckoned enthusiastically with her hand. I looked beyond at one of my neighboring campsites. Two men were busying themselves around a picnic table. Pots steamed from a giant Coleman camper stove.

"Moon Festival?" I asked.

"Come," she laughed and turned to lead me to the campsite. I grabbed a few cans of smoked salmon to contribute to any potential feast and followed. I entered the new campsite and the two men smiled. The lady turned to me.

"I am Jennifer. This is mah husband Xi and this is father, Chun Kon." She introduced me to the smiling, bespectacled men.

"Pleasure, I am Norris," I shook their hands. I put my cans of salmon on the table. "I brought these for you," I said. The father started to give them back, but I insisted they keep them. It was principle. I mingled and my jaw dropped at the spread. A plate towered with strange buns and thick noodles slathered in a soup loaded with meatballs and greens. The trio talked pleasantly in Chinese and sometimes tried to talk with me in English. The father was particularly interested and mimed a moose they saw by making antlers out of his hands.

"I was a *fisher*-man," I wiggled my arms and made a fish face by sucking in my cheeks and popping my eyes. The old man looked to Jennifer and she spoke to him in Chinese. He laughed and pointed to the cans I had given them. "Yeah! Fish!" The soup was ladled out and I was part of the family. The buns had some kind of delicious, salty seed paste in the center. I was in heaven.

"Do you eat like this every day? What a feast," I said.

"I'm sorry?" Jennifer leaned her ear in. I pointed to the table.

"Good food!" I gestured. She made an "ah-ha" face and nodded.

"Yes, Moon Festival today. Very important for Chinese culture. Very important to be kind," Jennifer said. We enjoyed each other's company for another hour or so. The father was a riot, full of laughter as he reenacted hiking and bears. I asked and they had not seen any wolves. No such luck. I dismissed myself as the night crept in. Jennifer gave me a hug.

"You very brave, please be careful," she said. The father spoke in Chinese when I shook his hand.

"What did he say?" I asked Jennifer.

"He say he don't wan to see you on the news," Jennifer said. They were leaving in the morning and gave me the firewood they no longer needed. I returned to my picnic bench in high spirits, despite the lack of shelter. It was the Moon Festival, after all. How could I be upset?

I stood on the bank of Hines Creek, campground behind and backcountry ahead. My loyal Coyote 4500 on my back held my supplies, some of which were rentals. I carried wet canned foods like chili, not the kind of thing the pros take out but I figured I could muscle the extra weight. The impromptu tutorial from the outdoor staff for my rental Whisper Light backpacking stove was fresh in my mind. I glanced at my government-issue topo map and had a good idea about how the next three days in the backcountry were supposed to go.

The season was officially over, one only had to look around at the abandoned tourist town outside the park entrance for proof. Bins of five-dollar clearance souvenirs littered the walkway outside the shops. I bought a foldable Kershaw knife with a metallic red handle that looked pink under most lighting. It was pathetically small and not good for much, but at least I had something. Jane of Jane's Knives would've been ashamed.

The ranger I checked in with assigned me a camping zone close to the park entrance because the shuttles to the interior were closed for the year. He said I was the only one in my zone. I was not to venture into an area marked red on the map on the edge of my territory.

"That is a wolf rendezvous," the ranger said and pointed it out on the topo map.

"Rendezvous?" I asked.

"The pack gathers there with the pups and teaches them life skills, like how to hunt," he explained. Was I at last to see a wolf? Wolf sighting stories had taunted me since big Bob's story on the flight to Cordova, and what started as persistent curiosity had simmered into a deep yearning. In that moment with the topo map in my hand and thoughts still reeling from the events of the summer, the feeling that encountering the wolves would lead to some greater enlightenment became all encompassing. Logic be dammed, the answer to the persistent Why with a capital w surely had something to do with this fated rendezvous with these so-far elusive animals. No pressure, lupines.

I promised the ranger not to enter the wolves' territory, but I schemed to hike along its border. I watched a mandatory video about bear attacks, was issued my bear-proof canister for my food, signed some paper, forked over a few bucks, and was dialed in for my trip.

"This is it," I muttered and stepped into the creek, a quaint first obstacle a few inches deep. I conquered it easily and tackled the steep riverbank on the other side. It was a scramble, but when I stood on top of it I let loose a satisfied huff. I turned to the forest of lichen-encrusted pine and spongy, moss-covered soil. I moved to look at my map and froze.

Where is it?!

My gut wrenched and I spun around. I had dropped my map on the riverbank. It must've slipped a pocket. I hung my head and retrieved it. I looked around to see if anybody had seen me. There were no witnesses. I guess that was kind of the point.

The terrain of the taiga forest was not to my liking. Thin, scraggly pines and brushy undergrowth made for a claustrophobe's nightmare. I fell onto a small path that wound about for no discernable reason and reckoned it was a game trail. This made the dark forest more foreboding, for the last thing I wanted to do was stumble upon a grizzly or a moose in close quarters.

Snap! I froze at a twig's outburst. The underbrush to my right moved, disturbed by something my size or larger. I straightened to face whatever it was. One hand drifted to the snap of my backpack's waist strap, the other to my tiny knife clipped to my shoulder strap. If a moose charged at me, I'd ditch the pack and make a break for it. Bear, I was to make a stand. My knife was cheap and small, but I knew I could poke an eye with it.

Snap! The thing drew closer.

Snap! Now was the time to make my presence known.

"Heyyy, bear. Heyyy, bear, bear," I called, my voice loud but friendly. A verbal olive branch.

"Oh hey there, I'm not a bear, eh," a friendly, decidedly Canadian voice answered. I sucked in a deep breath while two backpackers in their late twenties emerged from the vegetation. They both wore dirty packs and sported dark, scraggly beards and wool beanies. Pros.

"Heading out of here?" I asked the Canadian dirtbags. I was still pretty close to the park entrance.

"Oh yeah. We were just having a look aboot. Shame we missed the shuttle season, eh?" One of them said.

"Yup, oh well," I replied and pointed my chin ahead. "See anything big?"

"Oh no, we haven't seen anything. Just a little day trek," the other said. We stood in silence for a few seconds, our hands idling at our shoulder straps.

"Well, nice meeting ya," the first one said. We parted ways. It was reassuring to see a couple of people doing what I was doing, but as soon as I couldn't hear them anymore, the fearful hyper awareness took hold again. My footfalls were quiet when I walked over moss or soil, but sometimes I stepped on a stick or pushed through brush.

Snap! My noise made me cringe. A jay yelled at me and I jogged away, my head hung in frightened shame. I hiked at a brisk pace along the game trail when I stepped on a bloody moose antler. I reached down to pick it up. A young buck had left it, but it struck me odd that a moose's antler would be shed now during the rut. The males needed their antlers to win mates. Did it snap off? Trauma wound? I held up the puzzle. A perfect bite was taken out of the palm.

Bear.

I scanned the forest. A hole wide enough for me to scoot in on my belly sat ten paces to my right. Bones littered the pitch-black entrance. My blood ran cold.

A den?

I dropped the antler and continued as fast as I could along a river for a couple of hours until the sunlight started to wane. The river wasn't only my talking companion, but also my guide. She'd lead me out of the park if I needed and was a ready supply of fresh water. Hikers call features that serve this purpose handrails. The river and I were pretty great pals, and I decided to camp by her at the end of the long day of hiking.

The ranger taught me the Magic Triangle Formation for bear country and I started to set it up. I pitched my tent a hundred paces upwind of where I ate, kept my used dishes and toiletries, and brushed my teeth. I then completed the equilateral triangle by storing my bear can of food a hundred paces from the other two points and downwind of my tent. I ate a can of chili with crackers, boiled some water to replenish my stores for the next day, and cleaned it all as the sun set. I huddled in my tent and resolved not to leave it for the night.

My primary goal for the next day was to leave the river's comforting bosom in favor of higher, more open ground. If I could get off the game trails and out of the dense taiga forest, I'd be ok. I eyed the restricted zone of the wolf rendezvous and contemplated a route that would take me to its borders.

Light rain made music on the rainfly and my eyelids grew heavy. I thought of Chris McCandless in his magic bus that wasn't too far from where I was near the Talkeetna River. He who had been without fear. He who was dead.

The day's climb stretched before me, slopes covered in tundra lichens and mosses. Trees became sparse and brush clumped in the dips of the terrain where the wind wasn't so savage and mountain runoff flowed. Cold air whipped through my mop of hair and cut my lungs. My pack was too heavy, in part due to the cans of chili and extra bottles of surplus water I carried. A true alpine-style trekker would've sniggered at me.

My sea legs weren't used to this type of exertion and the deckhand strength of my chest and arms was dead weight. I spat thick foamy wads of saliva. The beginnings of a headache radiated over my skull. My face flushed. I took a break and half-collapsed onto the ground. I couldn't have climbed more than 1,000 feet, but it had been straight up through the bush. There was still further to go.

I looked back at the river and the thick forest that hugged her. I felt safer up here where I could see everything for miles. Squat orange and black butterflies fluttered around me. One landed on my face to lap up my sweat. This spot didn't seem so bad and I was tempted to call it a premature day when the cry of a red-tailed hawk rose me to my feet. The bird of prey rode a thermal overhead and floated past me, deeper into the park. I realized I was to follow her. I spent most of my summer, and life, being told where to be and when, and I had a hunch that the adult world wasn't much different.

When else could I choose to follow a hawk's cry? I pushed on long after the hawk vanished over the peaks above me.

Those heights were not like the sharp teeth of the Chugach Mountains around Cordova, but rather massive, undulating ridges that formed pockets for alpine lakes and river valleys. The terrain bounced up and down like that until Mt. Denali took charge on the horizon, hidden by clouds but undeniably there.

The sun threatened to set and I was finally satisfied with my progress. I set up my tent, a piece of cake, and marched downwind with the bear can. I hid my stash in a stump and turned about, my head down to pick my way over the spongy lichen.

I glanced at my tent and gasped. A young bull moose emerged from the far brush, his antlers relatively small on his massive head. How such a gigantic animal moved so quietly was beyond belief, but the doll-eyed, draft horse-sized creature casually picked his way downhill to within twenty feet of my tent. I just started to wonder whether I should give him a call of "hey moose" so I wouldn't surprise him, when the fella began to bawl a serious of low, piteous bellows.

Another moose emerged from the top of the hill. This one had a much larger rack. His flaccid dewlap swung with every lanky step on knobby legs. He marched down the hill toward the smaller one who whined.

The rut.

I thought the big one's focus was undivided, so I chanced a few steps toward my tent. His gaze snapped onto me and he snorted. I held my breath. He glowered at me and stomped a hoof.

"Heyyy moose," I said softly as we stood off. My knees bent, ready to sprint. I heard that bears could charge for any number of reasons, the least likely of which being with the intent to kill. Moose were different. A moose charge was serious business.

He sized me up for a minute before he continued down the slope to bully his rival. I was not a threat to his sex life. I breathed again and inched forward after the pair of them descended to a safer distance. The two moose made circles around one another.

"Fight, fight, fight," I whispered under my breath, hoping for a duel. But the conflict was resolved with the little fella surrendering, the typical conclusion. He made a break for it downslope while the big one menaced his heels.

I stretched out on the lichen blanket and watched the sun go down. A hawk owl buzzed me and perched in a nearby tree while I ate chili out of the can, satisfied with lightening my load while nourishing myself. It wasn't as overcast as the previous night and the stars came out in uncensored glory.

Tomorrow was an ambitious day. I hatched a plan for my escape out of the backcountry. I was to climb to the top and follow the ridge's edge, a natural road that curved to the border of the wolf rendezvous and back toward the campground. Then I would descend through the forest, find a creek handrail, and follow it back to the camping area. Finally, I'd pitch there for the night and figure out the next step. I was anxious for my wolf meeting and the important lesson that was sure to follow.

Lesson of the Wolf

I climbed until I left the trees and lichens behind. The ridgeline I walked upon was steep. At times I only had an arm span of walkable ground between cliffs that fell to both sides. The wind howled like the wolves I hope to see, and I was forced to take a knee and hold onto the ground for fear of being pried off my ridge-top highway. The clouds brought by the wolf wind shrouded my world grey. I had spent two days going into the park. If I was to get out in one, I couldn't afford delays.

I rose to my feet and continued my march. Tiny shards of ice stung my cheeks, but the frigid grip of the morning began to loosen. The clouds burned away under the onslaught of the sun's golden arrows. The landscape below me, once drab under the oppression of the cold rain, caught fire with yellows, reds, oranges, and browns. Fall on the tundra. The wind lessened and ridgetop leveled.

I continued along the ridge-top highway until I came upon a ram Dall sheep walking toward me. He walked the mountain road as I did, and I felt both validated that my technique of ridgetop travel was used by the pros and worried that he would knock me off the cliff to my right. The ram was a full curler, not one to be messed with, and stopped a hundred feet from me. I held my ground and hoped he would detour around me. He didn't budge and stared me down with raised chin.

"Eh?" I gestured suggestively to my left where the ridge sloped into a shallow bowl.

Two minutes passed.

I scowled and crossed my arms. He didn't move.

Another two minutes passed.

I shivered in the biting wind. He didn't even twitch. I wagged my finger at him.

"Come on, you can let me pass, can't you?" I asked. The ram could've been a stone carving. I stood for another two minutes. Nothing changed. I wondered if these things attacked.

"Fine," I threw up my hands and carefully scrambled down the left basin. I took about twenty paces before he resumed his walk past me. I gave him a head start and returned to the ridgeline to watch him. He leapt off the cliff. I gasped as I leaned over to see his acrobatics in action. He joined four ewes, his ladies, who were perched on the cliff face. I had walked right over them.

"Ah, that makes sense," I said and continued on my way, not a threat to yet another wild beast's sex life. "Lucky guy."

I pushed on for several more hours until I stood upon the rim of a valley colored by the tundra quilt. Pine trees grew around a dark blue lake cradled by the cliffs. I shed my pack to check my topo map and compass. Yes, this was the place. The wolf rendezvous.

I scanned the landscape with my binoculars, thirsty for a glimpse of the wolves whose guidance I sorely needed. I thought of big Bob's hunting story about the black wolf during the flight to Cordova and the book *Ordinary Wolves* I had read at Hawk House. I remembered Kara's story of the lone wolf wandering Larry's mushroom hunting grounds and of the music in the wind that sounded like their howling. Zoe the dog's calm, intense gaze was just a teaser for what was to come. This mythical animal had been with me since the beginning of my journey in every way but physical presence. I wanted to change that. Needed to change that. I lowered the binoculars after my sweat cooled.

There were no wolves.

I cupped my hands to my mouth and let fly my best wolf howl. It died on the wind with only an echo for a response. I waited, alone.

If there were no wolves in the valley, what was the point? Why was I here, alone on a barren ridge in the middle of nowhere? Why had I gone through all I had, seen all I had seen? There had to be a purpose to it all, a reason I chose this strange and difficult path. The wolf had some answer to give me. I needed that answer.

I kicked my pack before I threw my arms back to shout at the top of my lungs.

I stopped when my voice cracked.

Silence.

Why did I come to Alaska? Why was May Wood dying of cancer? Why did Captain Edmond sing opera? What was Anthony going to write in his new journal? For what did I endure? Surely, the wolf had the answer. The wolf, once revealed, would help me make sense of it all. Something important would happen. I closed my eyes and dug into my guts. All the triumphs and failures of my life rose in a single desperate cry. Images flashed past like projector slides. Tears fell.

The dream with the salmon people.

Seiners floating in cold misty heaven.

Walking Alice home from the pet store.

Scott a rag doll in the deck winch.

The thudding of helicopter blades.

"Was dad hurt?" Anthony held up the bloody Spiderman blanket. "Yes baby."

Man is fish. Fish is man. Salt and blood and sperm and egg. I gasped for breath and sank to my knees, light-headed from yelling. Spit ran down my chin and my heart pounded in my ears. My desperate echoes quieted. I scanned the valley one last time for the wolf. Many silent minutes slipped by. I was alone.

The day was long in the tooth when I emerged from the mountains to begin the downhill trek out of the park. The going was swift over the tundra sponge. I passed through a sculpture garden of petrified trolls, likely boulders dropped from an Ice Age glacier. I could see a landmark creek below, my handrail to the campground. A dark forest of scraggly black spruce was a final obstacle and I charged into the shadowy scrub. My hike quickly turned into a desperate wrestling match. Branches grabbed at me and I made painfully slow progress by bullying my way down the hill.

Crack! Snap!

I broke the brooding silence of the place.

Snap!

Something made a noise in the woods to my right. I froze.

"Heyyy, bear! Hey, bear!" I called, hoarse. Whatever it was never showed. I could barely see the light through the dense canopy, but the sun was not far from setting. I had no compass bearing anymore. All I knew was that downhill should lead me to the creek. My guide.

Crack!

I sucked on a fresh cut to the back of my hand and stumbled on. A patch of mud surprised me and I slid onto my back.

Snap! Crack!

"I'm in hell," I snarled and lumbered back to my feet. I passed a felled aspen. Had I seen this one before? Fear crept around me like the growing shadows of the dying day. I paused on the edge of tears to collect myself, more lost now than I had ever been.

A sound caught my attention. I strained my ears in disbelief. Dogs were barking.

The ranger station?

I knew the Denali National Park Service maintained a facility of working sled dogs a mile or so into the park, so I doubled my efforts in the direction of the barking. An hour or two passed before I crashed through the final stand of trees and stood at the edge of the creek I sought. The dog kennels were on a high bank across the water. I wished I could give each of those noble pooches a giant bone to chew on.

Exhausted, I sank onto a log by the brook, relieved to nearly be out of the woods. I wasn't going to beat the night, but at least I was in the home stretch to the campground. I dunked my head into a glacial melt baptism and emerged refreshed. My breathing levelled. Almost as an afterthought, I realized I knew all that I needed to know, wolf or no wolf. I saw the first stars of the Alaskan night for what they were, not what I wanted them to be, and tried to decipher the many animal tracks in the mud around me to learn their stories.

A single wolf pawprint the size of my open hand lay, perfect, beside my own.

EPILOGUE – SALMON IN THE SEINE

I was fresh from the woods and hovering near a pair of gas station pumps when I thumbed my first ride as a bone fide hitchhiker. I harbored doubts the system worked as advertised, but I wasn't at it long before a gigantic beast of a black truck pulled up. The driver looked to be in his mid-thirties with a shaved head, a more diesel look than a combover for a balding man. He pointed at me through the open passenger window with a tattooed arm. Uncle Sam's biker cousin.

"You!" he hollered as his ride ground to a halt at the pumps. I lowered my thumb and approached. He was a bit shorter than me with small gold earrings. "Name's Toby," he gave my hand a good thrashing in greeting.

"I'm Norris."

"Fairbanks?" Toby asked.

"You got it," I said. I pitched the pack in the bed and we were off. My grin faltered when I noticed the colossal pistol on the dashboard. Toby saw my gaze.

"Fifty-caliber," he declared.

"Fifty! What for?" I asked.

"Well, once I hit a moose with the truck and, damn, an injured moose is a sad and dangerous thing. This baby will take care of the next one, no problemo." Toby was a seasonal bar manager at one of the lodges in the Denali tourist town. "Good money and plenty of adventurous young people for the season looking to get laid. And you've got this great outdoor playground! Do you four wheel?"

"Can't say I have," I said.

"Dude, you're missing out," he said. "I almost fuck'n died trying to four wheel across the Talkeetna River just over yonder. I would've seen the *Into the Wild* kid's magic bus if I made it. I guess a lot of people get in trouble trying to find it—like me, ha!"

Neither of us could've predicted it at the time, but the magic bus would ultimately find a home in Fairbanks at the superb Museum of the North in the far-off year of 2020. If we were willing not only to get to Fairbanks but hold position for twelve years, we'd see the bus for the price of a museum admission ticket and be spared the currency of life and limb.

Toby turned to me. "That kid was alright. You four-twenty friendly?"

"Four... huh?" I asked. Toby took a hit from an imaginary joint. "Oh, nah I'm good. Go ahead though." We burned up that lonely road to Fairbanks alright, speed limits be dammed. Toby lit up, took a hero's hit, and belched smoke. Very little of the haze made it out of the window. I watched trees with their autumn colors go by for a while and relaxed in a gentle secondhand high.

"So what's your deal, bud? What brings you up this way?" Toby asked.

"I worked the season as a commercial fisherman out of Cordova. Deckhand on a seiner chasing humpies. I thought I'd check out Denali and maybe see some wolves."

"Word," Toby said as he exhaled dragon breath. I took a few minutes to appreciate that, somehow, this leap of faith summer made me flush with cash. I had the rest of the year before college to spend as I pleased. The intoxicating possibilities swirled in my mind like the marijuana smoke filling the truck.

"I'm just kind of a salmon in the seine, ya know?" I said.

"What do you mean by that?" He asked. I shrugged, not entirely sure.

Photographer credit: Jonathan Cooper

ABOUT THE AUTHOR

Salmon in the Seine is Norris's first book. Between gigs at sea, the Pacific Northwest-based author writes for magazines and the highest bidder. He holds a B.S. in Marine Science, won five Boat Writers International awards, received honorable mention for the annual *Writer's Digest* writing competition, and was a contestant on Season 5 of the Norwegian Reality TV show, *Alt for Norge*.

Thank you for supporting the creative works of veterans and military family members by purchasing this book. If you enjoyed your reading experience, we're certain you'll enjoy these other great reads.

CRY OF THE HEART
by RLynn Johnson

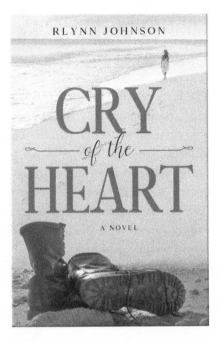

After law school, a group of women calling themselves the Alphas embark on diverse legal careers—Pauline joins the Army as a Judge Advocate. For twenty years, the Alphas gather for annual weekend retreats where the shenanigans and truth-telling will test and transform the bonds of sisterhood.

SUB WIFE
by Samantha Otto Brown

A Navy wife's account of life within the super-secret sector of the submarine community, and of the support among spouses who often wait and worry through long stretches of silence from loved ones who are deeply submerged.

BEYOND THEIR LIMITS OF LONGING
by Jennifer Orth-Veillon

The first collection of poetry, fiction, and nonfiction to reveal the important, yet often overlooked, influence of World War One on contemporary writers and scholars— many of them post-911 veterans. Among the contributors are Pulitzer Prize-winning and National Book Award-winning authors.

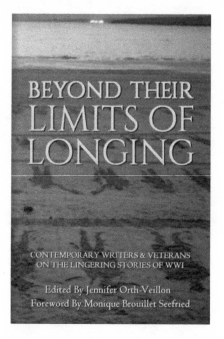

COLLATERAL DAMAGE 2ND EDITION
by Kevin C. Jones

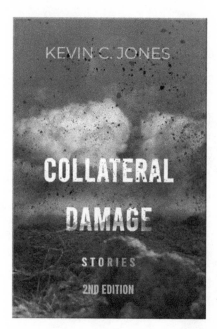

These stories live in the real-world psychedelics of warfare, poverty, love, hate, and just trying to get by. Jones's evocative language, the high stakes, and heartfelt characters create worlds of wonder and grace. The explosions, real and psychological, have a burning effect on the reader. Nothing here is easy, but so much is gained.
—Anthony Swofford, author of Jarhead: A Marine's Chronicle of the Gulf War and Other Battles

CPSIA information can be obtained
at www.ICGtesting.com
Printed in the USA
JSHW010750220922
30843JS00003B/17